A VERY PRESTON AFFAIR

*the tale of a School and a Square
... and of some who were there*

DAVID 'CHARLIE' BILLINGTON

Published privately by Preston Grammar School Association
to celebrate its longevity and to commemorate its inevitable closure
on the fiftieth anniversary of the demise of the School

ISBN 978-1-5272-6783-1 Paperback

A CIP catalogue record for this book is available from the British Library

Design, typesetting and prepress production pro bono by Andrew Mather
with assistance from Christine Beatty AMA DataSet Ltd, Preston
Cover painting of the Preston Grammar School by Robin Utracik, Preston

Printed by Charlesworth Press, Wakefield

PERSONAL DEDICATION

**This booklet is dedicated to the memory of
Preston Grammar School
and its Association**

In particular, inter alia,
Bernard John Moody (Headmaster PGS 1962–66),
John Woodall, Ron Foreman (Modern Languages), Ted Dewhurst (Maths),
and H. N. B. (Nigel) Morgan, History Master, local historian and friend.

Also John Brandwood and John Paterson (English),
late stalwarts of the Association and
Jim Bryson, former Member of the PGSA Executive Council,
long-time Secretary of the Preston Referees Society
and colleague and Friend of Steve Harrison (see Foreword) and the author.

Preston Grammar School c.1900

Print from a postcard by the late Ron Severs (PGSA)

CONTENTS

FOREWORD

My time at Preston Grammar School overlapped with that of David (Charlie) Billington. We were later at the same University at the same time. Our paths crossed over the decades in serendipitous ways. Work took me away from Lancashire from the mid-1990s until my wife and I decided to move back to Preston and find a place to live close to the centre of town.

I became a founder member of the Friends of Winckley Square (FoWS); a group of volunteers which aims to explore the heritage of the Square and promote its conservation, enhancement and future usage (www.winckleysquarepreston.org).

When I came back to Preston 'Charlie' recruited me to the Preston Grammar School Association. Our interests and activities once again overlapped. As members of FoWS research the Square's history and impact on the development of Preston, time and again the Grammar School features. The physical impact was the buildings on Stoneygate and Cross Street. The human impact is through those connected with the Square who taught at or who attended the School and those who made decisions about its move from Stoneygate to what Marian Roberts described as one of three 'handsome buildings' along with the Winckley Club and the Literary & Philosophical Society.

These links are like the warp and weft of the finest Horrockses' cloth. The Houses that all pupils after 1911 belonged to were drawn from the era when the Square was at the heart of the political and social life of Preston. Miller, named after the cotton magnate who built the mansion at No 5 Winckley Square. As rich as Croesus, he donated the land for the park that bears his name but was the leading light in the Cotton Masters' defeat of the workers in the great lock out of 1853/54 which inspired Dickens to write *Hard Times*. Goodair (something else Charlie and I shared), named after John Goodair, also a cotton manufacturer but one who refused to join the Masters' Association in locking out the workforce. Harris, the family name of the great philanthropist Edmund Robert Harris (son of one of the least effective Headmasters of the school) whose legacy is still reflected in the Harris Museum, Art Gallery and Library, in UCLan and, within the Winckley Square Quarter, in the magnificent but neglected Avenham Institute. Finally there was Thornley House. Named after Edmund Thornley, Grocer and Wine merchant of Latham Street, south of Winckley Square.

Sometimes the connections are surprising. Susan Douglass, an old girl of the Park School, researched Louisa Frances Walsh, the first headmistress of the Preston High School for Girls. Susan wrote about the ill treatment of Miss Walsh by the

Headmaster of PGS, the Rev Alfred Beaven Beaven (so good they named him twice). Beaven might not have been as poor a Headmaster as the Rev Harris but if you read Susan's story you will probably conclude he was a man you would never have tired of punching.

Finally, these connections include the work of Nigel Morgan, History Master at PGS and later historian of Preston's social history. Nigel taught me as a pupil and later as a postgraduate. His work on Preston in the nineteenth century is a key source for anyone who wants to understand the growth of the town and how it came to top the national league table for infant mortality year after year. Nigel wrote extensively about Winckley Square. His last volume *Desirable Dwellings* has been published online on the excellent Preston History website (prestonhistory. com/subjects/desirable-dwellings/) thanks to Peter Smith, another former pupil taught by Nigel.

It's worth recalling too that in 1907 when Cross Street was no longer deemed suitable as a location for the town's Grammar School the favoured option was to build a replacement above the Ribble near Bank Parade and Avenham Park. Instead Moor Park was chosen. Had the decision gone the other way PGS would have joined the Catholic College, Winckley Square Convent and the precursor to the Park School in the heart of the town. The journey to the sports fields would certainly have been shorter.

Charlie's work on the history of the Grammar School is another piece of the jigsaw which, along with work being carried out by groups and individuals, provides us with insights into our history and our local heritage and it reminds us that what may seem at first glance to be rather parochial is nothing of the kind. This publication is a welcome addition to our knowledge and understanding of our shared past. I congratulate Charlie on his research and his commitment to the legacy of the School.

Steve Harrison, Friends of Winckley Square

INTRODUCTION

Historical processes involve the interaction of structures, institutions and individual biographies and this observation is as true of local history as it is of national history. In the present work, Mr Billington has paid due attention to all these aspects. He presents us with what is in effect a history of Preston Grammar School in terms of its physical environment before its departure from its historic site on Cross Street to the new Moor Park site just before the outbreak of the First World War.

He begins with a short sketch of the prehistory of the school and its association with Preston Guild, though he is well aware of the difficulties involved in assessing the source material from the medieval period. The main body of his work is concerned with the history of the school and its architecture in the Winckley Square/Cross Street period in the nineteenth and early twentieth centuries. The detailed biographical sketches of Grammar School luminaries of this period are a fascinating piece of social history. In particular, the biographies of Old Boys like Captain Cedric Naylor, who was a notable naval commander involved in the fight against German submarines in the First World War, and Clive Whittle, one of the original Preston Pals, who was killed at Bazentin-le-Petit (Département Somme) in July 1916, allow local history to merge into the larger picture of national and indeed European history.

Preston Grammar School made a notable contribution to the intellectual life of the town and right up to its demise in 1969, it continued to produce outstanding public servants, architects, businessmen and academics. My own way took me from Preston to Cambridge, Nottingham, Erlangen, Berlin and Heidelberg and I am grateful for the sound training I received from the Masters at the Grammar School, in particular from the late H. N. B. Morgan, who set me on the path of medieval studies which I have followed ever since. That the fate of the school was sealed by the stroke of a pen in April 1964 by Tuson's *Reappraisal of the Organisation of Secondary Education in Preston* was a tragedy whose consequences are still being felt. Mr Billington is to be congratulated for having produced a fitting memorial to the school in its Winckley Square/Cross Street days. A further volume covering the history of the school in its Moor Park days would be most appropriate and greatly appreciated.

Professor John Insley, University of Heidelberg
English Place-Name Society, Editor for Lancashire

PRESTON GRAMMAR SCHOOL
AND WINCKLEY SQUARE

Author's Foreword

When asked to contribute an article on Preston Grammar School to a recent book about Winckley Square as Secretary of the Old Boys' Association,* I readily agreed but two things immediately struck me. Firstly the School was not in Winckley Square until the Literary and Philosophical Society building was annexed in 1898 and secondly a lot of research would be required as there was a relative lack of information, reliable or otherwise. But there was no doubt that a mutual relationship did exist between the School and the Square and with the imminent demise of the Association it was the perfect opportunity to present a monograph written by an Old Boy for Old Boys, or indeed anyone with an interest in local history or a good story, in dedication to the memory of the Preston Grammar School and its Association, as well as all the Masters and boys who attended the School over many hundreds of years. The article was condensed from this text, which though well-researched and wide-ranging, has a single theme and is not a linear history, this having been provided by Jim Heppell with his splendid book, *A History of Preston Grammar School*, over twenty years ago (see bibliography).

People are surprised to learn that despite the official closure of the Preston Grammar School in 1969, a thriving Association still exists, at least as I write, to maintain and uphold the memories, traditions and indeed the history of an institution that at one time offered so much and was held so dearly in Preston. The Association will be gone by the end of 2019, but it would be very unfair to airbrush the Grammar School out of any account of the social, political, historical and cultural development of the town (now city), itself a monumental narrative that along the way reserves a special place for Winckley Square and inextricably links it with the School. It is also true to say that in the case of the School, Winckley Square, although important, is but a chapter in a monumental tome.

That the Association has survived for fifty years beyond the closure of the School is testament to its members and in particular to those who have been prepared, nay keen, to put in the work required to maintain it. In my time I have enjoyed the Presidencies of Stephen Sartin, Tony Olivine, Mike Tyrer, the Centenary President John Brandwood (who was also the 1972 Guild President), the long-serving John Mayson Whalley and Jim Goring. The supporting cast has been the officials and the Executive Council, which used to number over thirty but now consists only of five;

Jim Goring (President), Brian Hall (Treasurer), Brian Rigby (Archivist), Trevor Sergeant (Trips) and myself (Secretary). To each and everyone past and present I offer my heartfelt thanks, and in particular the current Council for supporting the financing of this monograph, the proceeds of which will go in their entirety to St Catherine's Hospice. We've all been touched by cancer and the Hospice does a truly wonderful job.

It's sad that the Association is about to close down, but many of us will stay in touch, we're going out on a high and we've had a tremendous innings! It was even sadder in 1969 that the Grammar School closed as this was involuntary. Whilst the decision was obviously welcomed in some quarters it was not in others, where many viewed it as an act of political vandalism in pursuit of an ideology that continues to divide opinion even today. In 1972, for the first time in centuries, there was no Grammar School presence at the Preston Guild. However, one reason the Association has continued to thrive, particularly latterly, has been the good relationship with the staff of the Moor Park High School and Sixth Form, which has allowed us amongst other things to carry out an annual visit to our alma mater, which, with its sympathetic restorations and renovations, remains eminently recognisable to any Old Boy! It also houses a number of artefacts from the old Cross Street Grammar School.

Shame about the building...

David 'Charlie' Billington
December 2019

---

* Eds. Andrew Mather, Alan Crosby and Aidan Turner-Bishop, *A Portrait of Winckley Square, Preston*, Winckley Square Press, Preston 2018.

THE ORIGINS OF
THE GRAMMAR SCHOOL
IN PRESTON

To fully understand the origins of the Grammar School and its relevance to Preston and the cultural movements that along the way embraced Winckley Square, it is important to consider the Guild Merchant. In the nineteenth century some Guilds were held in difficult times, such as 1842 (riots and shootings) and 1862 (the cotton famine). This could be extended to 1902 (the Boer War) and 1922 (the aftermath of the Great War). The Guild Celebration was, and is, a permanent institution in the history of Preston, and in recent centuries its sequence has been interrupted only once, in 1942 by the Second World War. Despite the arrival of free trade in the eighteenth century the tradition has remained firmly entrenched, and the celebration is the only one left of its kind in the United Kingdom.

Guilds originated in Anglo-Saxon times, when a growth in population necessitated their formation for mutual personal assistance and protection. As trade and wealth increased, religious Guilds and then secular or trading Guilds (Gilda Mercatoria) came into being. If a borough was granted a Gilda Mercatoria or Guild Merchant, its inhabitants had the exclusive right to trade within the borough, and the right to set up a department of town administration which maintained and regulated the trade monopoly. A fully paid-up individual who had sworn allegiance to the Mayor and the Merchant would gain admittance to the trade membership as a Burgess.

Preston existed in Anglo-Saxon times, and a church is recorded (in Amounderness) in the Domesday Book, so it is not unreasonable to surmise that the Preston Guild may have had some very early origins. Records show that in 1100 Preston was already recognised as a free borough and this status may have been underpinned by an administrative structure.

The right to hold a Guild Merchant was conferred upon the Burgesses of Preston in Henry II's Charter of 1179, and although it is assumed that this right would have been exercised in the ensuing 150 years (previous records may have been destroyed when Robert the Bruce 'burnt' Preston in 1322), it is not until 1328 that there is a trustworthy record of such a celebration. It was then that it was decreed that a 'guild' should be held every twenty years rather than annually/frequently, as the membership renewal of Burgesses would be required only on a generational basis, the alternative being chaos. Nonetheless ensuing Guilds appear to have remained

The Chapter House, Cockersand Abbey
Photograph by the author

somewhat irregular until 1542, whence there commenced a sequence unbroken to the present day, notwithstanding 1942. An ironic twist here is that this Guild, delayed by ten years, was celebrated without the Guild (Town) Hall, as it had been destroyed not by the War but by the disastrous fire of 1947.

It is inconceivable that Preston, with its strong guilds (and precursors?) from an early date and the increasing growth in trade, would not have required a decent level of literacy and numeracy amongst its Burgesses. And it was a secular guild, hence the need for a 'grammar' education in some form or other. Whilst this is speculative, hard evidence both for the Guild and the School being hard to come by, in 1358 there is a direct reference to one 'John le Clerk of Broghton, Magister, the Schoolmaster of Preston', who, with others and following the proclamation of a pardon for a murder previously committed by a Nicholas Starkie, was charged with causing a riot in the Chapel of St Mary Magdalene (near to where St Walburge's Church now stands).

In 1397 a Richard Marshall appears on the Guild Roll having been admitted as a foreign Burgess, and two years later, in 1399 (1400 with the current calendar), he was appointed master 'of the Grammar School', confirmed or licensed by the Archdeacon of Richmond. The 1415 Guild Roll describes him as 'Ricus Marschall, scolemaster.' And in 1474 Thomas Preston, Master of the School, received 'letters dimissory for orders' from Archbishop Neville of York.

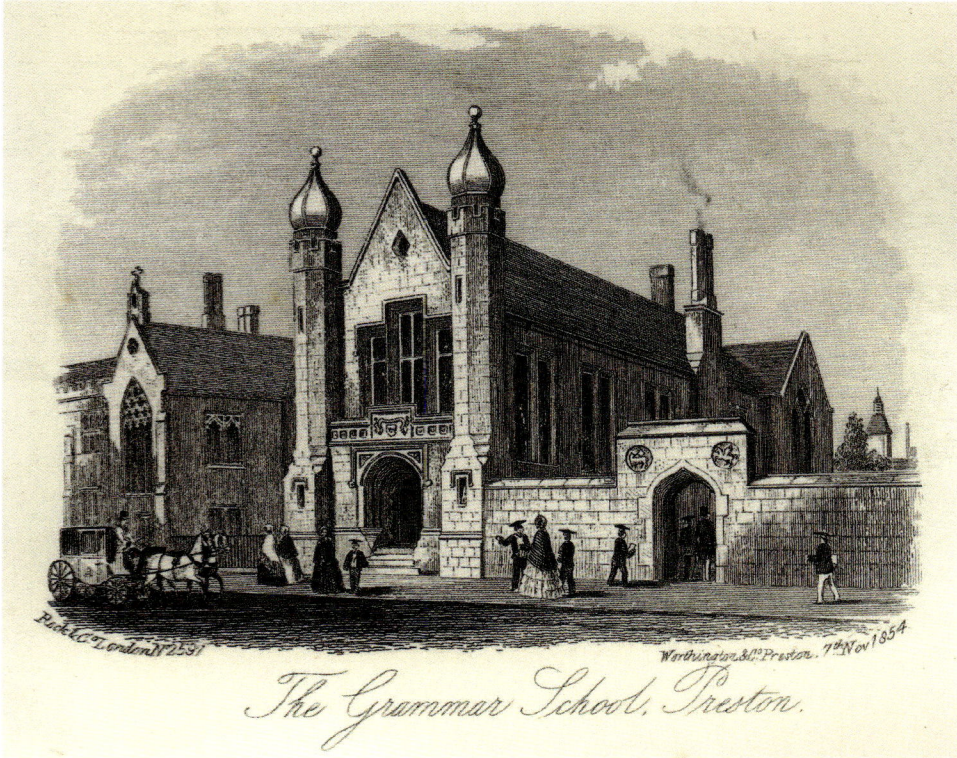

The Cross Street building in 1854 (Hardwick)
Preston Digital Archive (PDA)

There are perhaps even earlier references. Eleven charters (probably from 1230) are listed in the Chartulary of Cockersand Abbey and these grant pieces of land to a 'Magister Willelm de Kirkham'. His title would indicate that he was a University graduate and it has been suggested that he could have been Master of the Grammar School, the lands being transferred as an endowment for the School. Certainly in some of the charters it is recorded that the transfers were with the common assent of the whole town and confirmed by the Burgesses affixing the common seal. The case is possibly strengthened by the appointment some years later of Thomas de Kirkham (a son?) as 'Scholemaster' of Lancaster Grammar School.

Perhaps more conclusive and certainly more intriguing are the grants that specifically relate to the ditches of Gildhouse (9), St John's quarter (4 and 7) and St John the Baptist's quarter (8) in Preston. If this is the St John's area that we know today it includes Old Vicarage and Crooked Lane, where a building housed the Grammar School in the 1600s. And as we shall see there is a direct link between the Parish Church (now the Minster) and the Grammar School. We should not be put off by the reference to St John the Baptist. Whilst the Church was known as

St Wilfrid's, and would be up until the Reformation, the area near the Parish, and the Guild Celebration, were closely associated with St John the Baptist, who for a while was adopted as the Patron. From 1552 the Guild has traditionally commenced on the Monday after the Feast of the Decollation of St John the Baptist. Further, the Church dropped the dedication to St Wilfrid during the Reformation in favour of St John, possibly the Baptist and later possibly the Divine, for it finally to become St John the Evangelist as late as 1855. Such connections may justify further research, but meanwhile the underlying hypothesis remains a reasonable assumption.

Although the principle of a free 'grammar' school in Preston wasn't firmly established until the Hoghton Chantry of 1479 (this is an assumed date), there had obviously been some form of 'grammar' education going on for a long time, possibly centuries. The link between the need for education and the trading activities of the Burgesses was inextricable and continuous, as was the later link with cultural activities. When fee-paying was the norm at the Grammar School, Burgesses were still entitled to send their sons there at a reduced rate, and thus it remained until the Education Act of 1944, when entrance to the School became free of charge by examination.

The first reference to Grammar School boys participating in a Guild is in 1682, when on the first day the Mayor, Aldermen and Councillors marched between several Bars, in each of which they drank ale and heard a speech (presumably in Latin) by a scholar of the Grammar School. Having returned to the Market Cross, they all drank wine and the Headmaster gave a 'learned' speech, praising the King (Charles II) and his confirmation of the Guild Merchant. It was perhaps from this occasion that the custom arose of the Head Boy making a Latin oration during the Guild celebrations. If it ever fell out of favour, it was certainly revived in 1882. Twenty years later the Headmaster, H. C. Brooks, gave 'strict instructions' to all the boys, with Head Boy Richard Corless giving the Latin oration. Just what the 'strict instructions' were is not clear, but in more recent times (1952) Michael Knight, the Head Boy, was known to have prepared the oration and discussed it with the Latin Master, Mr H. T. Jones (affectionately known as 'Titus'), before copies were handed out to boys who could read Latin. Their task was to prompt applause at the right times!

In a stirring speech the last words spoken by Michael Knight were 'Vivat Regina; Floreat Ecclesia; Stet Fortuna Domus', which translate as 'Long Live the Queen; Let the Church Flourish; May the Fortune of the House Endure'. This was the School motto. The Recorder responded by praising the admirable training given in the Classics for more than 700 years by firstly 'Preston's famous Grammar School' and more recently the Park and other schools. The Guild Mayor, John James Ward, closed the proceedings by congratulating Michael Knight on 'his scholarly presentation of the Latin Oration which, by ancient custom, is always delivered by the Head Boy of the Grammar School'.

A decade later the Recorder's exhortation 'Vivat Schola Nobilis' had more than a hollow ring to it, as Preston's Grammar School was consigned to the political dustbin. For those who found this difficult to comprehend, the 1972 Guild provided little comfort but perhaps some closure. The resulting hiatus was not just about trade and education however, nor indeed about politics, for the School had for centuries been a key player in the development and maintenance of the culture of Preston, whether during or between Guilds. The bond between it, the Town, the Parish Church and the Guild Merchant had been incredibly strong. And for over seventy years its significance had manifested itself in the presence of a building near the very heart of the cultural movement in Preston, Winckley Square.

THE HOGHTON CHANTRY
AND STONEYGATE

Unlike the Park School (the Girls' Grammar School), which had a building in Winckley Square during the last century right up until its closure, the Boys' Grammar School only latterly had a physical presence in the exact part of Preston that would and did become the Square. However until 1913 it was never far away on account of its direct ties with the Parish Church. It is assumed that for some time the school was housed in a chapel within the Church, although there is strong evidence in a will to suggest that in the 1600s if not well before there was a building in Crooked Lane, probably associated with the old vicarage that gave its name to the way on which it was sited. However this does not detract from the fact that the School was never more than a stone's throw away from the political, economic, social and cultural activities of the town as well as the religious activity to which it owed its continued existence.

In the Middle Ages it was customary for pious people to establish Chantries by leaving money or land to provide for a chapel in a church, where a priest would say Mass and pray for the souls of the founder and his family. In 1450 Helen Masson married Henry Hoghton Esq of Hoghton at Preston Parish Church, although she was only classed as a concubine because the consent of Henry's father had not been obtained. However, following the latter's death, in 1468 Henry obtained a Papal Bull to legitimise the six children of the marriage, an indication that there was a good deal of wealth in the family. Thus some time after Henry's death in 1479 Helen (de Hoghton) established a Chantry at the altar of the Blessed Virgin Mary in Preston Parish Church, where a priest was not only expected to pray for all the souls concerned but also had to be 'sufficiently lerned in gramar to th'entent to have a fre gramar skole kept ther also, as by the seyd foundacion it doth appere'. The date of the foundation, 1479, is assumed as it is not known exactly when Helen died. Sometime later the Chantry passed into the possession of the Earls of Derby, but the close connection with the Parish Church was firmly established. Indeed, the priest or later vicar, was the priest or vicar to the Grammar School right through to its closure, and beyond that to the Grammar School Association.

There was soon to be conflict when in 1528 Roger Lewyns brought an action against the Mayor and Burgesses for trespass in turning him out of the Chantry. In his defence the Mayor pleaded that Lewyns had neglected an essential part of his duty, that of keeping a free school for the education of boys in Preston. The fundamental principle of the Chantry was duly upheld but ahead lay many more challenges.

Arkwright House c.1850

Watercolour by Preston artist Henry Pritt

With the Reformation the Chantries, as religious foundations, suffered the fate of the monasteries, though some survived as educational institutions, one being the Preston Grammar School, as proved by a charge of £2 16s 2d made during the reign of Edward VI on the revenues of the Duchy of Lancaster for the 'clerk and schoolmaster at Preston.' It does appear, however, that there may have been a bit of confusion as the Commissioners for the Dissolution of the Chantries stated in their report of 1548 that the conditions of Helen de Hoghton's bequest with regard to the School were still being observed. Indeed, there may have been two endowments connected with the School, the one provided by Helen de Hoghton and the other provided by the Corporation from around 1448 (or even possibly the early 1300s). However, following the abolition of the Chantry the School does not appear to have had any income apart from that provided by the Corporation, which precipitated many years of dispute, largely involving landowners, schoolmasters, and bailiffs as well as the Corporation.

The Restoration brought better days, for in 1663 the leasehold of a piece of land in Broadgate was bequeathed to the School by Bartholomew Worthington. The lease of the field, known as Johnson's Hey but afterwards called the School Field, was purchased by the Corporation and this ensured payment of the Headmaster's salary. Better still, three years later a new Grammar School building was erected on municipal land at the bottom of Stoneygate, near Syke Hill, described twenty years later as a 'remarkable Schoolhouse' by Dr Kuerden in his descriptive manuscripts. Of course the Syke, which ran behind the School, continued along the present

Cross Street and across Town End Field (now Winckley Square) before dropping down to the Ribble via the hollow below the site of the current railway station, established a direct physical link with the future Winckley Square long before the latter was even conceived. But it wasn't the first association, as the Register of St John's College, Cambridge for 1661 records that a 15-year-old boy, Elisha Clarkson, had been taught at the School by a Mr Winckley for the previous six years. Now there's a coincidence!

In 1728, financed by public subscription and the Council, a house was built close to the School in the Georgian style, to accommodate the Headmaster. This still stands, and during the course of its life it has had several incarnations. Occupied by Age Concern for the past thirty years, it has previously been a tavern, the *Arkwright Arms*, and a licensed lodging house, as well as an infamous 'doss house'. Arkwright House, to give it its current title, also has a more reputable claim to fame, for it was here in 1768 that the then Headmaster Ellis Henry gave permission for Richard Arkwright to use a back room to trial his water frame away from the prying eyes of the reactionaries who would have destroyed it. We might even claim that the Grammar School played a key role in the birth of the Industrial Revolution. Further, one of the last Headmasters to reside in the house (1788 to 1835) was the Rev Robert Harris BD, librarian of the Dr Richard Shepherd Library and father of Edmund Harris, the principal benefactor of the Harris Free Public Library and Museum, the Institute/Art School (now in private hands), the Technical School (now UCLAN) and the Orphanage (also in private hands).

On the face of it Stoneygate was the perfect site for the new buildings and indeed the Grammar School remained there for no less than 175 years. The two-storey Schoolhouse to which another building was added in 1690 was described by Dr Kuerden as 'remarkable', being 'large and hansom'. Francis Gantrell, Bishop of Chester at the beginning of the next century considered it noteworthy in an inventory of his diocese. However, in truth the actual wellbeing of the School was often beset by problems seemingly beyond the control of the Council.

Robert Oliver on his appointment as Headmaster in 1737 was already the Vicar of Warton-in-Lonsdale and he later obtained a third post (1744) as curate of St George's Church. His competing commitments meant that he was unable to give his full attention to the School, and to make matters worse in 1746, with complete disregard for the Council's Tory leanings, he preached a sermon (published in book form) at St George's in support of the Whig government of the day. A year later following a report it was decided to sack him on account of the state and condition of the School and the conduct of the Masters. It was noted that he made his own rules and chaos abounded as a result. The report stated that the School was greatly decayed and had lost its previous good reputation, so that many gentlemen and tradesmen sent their children out of town to other schools. Oliver's salary was suspended but he refused to leave either the job or the house and he apparently remained as Headmaster for another 17 years, being remunerated by his other posts, non-free scholars and 'cock-pennies' (traditionally given by pupils to pay for fighting cocks). He resigned without a contested back-pay award in 1764, becoming Vicar of St Michael's on Wyre and retaining his other two posts.

A year later he was replaced by Ellis Henry, who took possession of the house with Richard Shepherd as an incumbent tenant of the Council. He sublet other rooms to Richard Arkwright to presumably supplement his income, but this might also indicate a dearth of pupil boarders. After the death of the following Headmaster Thomas Fleetwood in 1788, Robert Harris was elected and he served for 47 years until 1835, the longest period of any Headmaster and generally an unhappy one.

As Curate of St George's Church from 1798 (and Vicar from 1844 until his death in 1862) Robert Harris was very popular with his parishioners and he did much to prepare Preston for social improvement. Possibly because of this he was not a successful Headmaster. Like Oliver before him he appears to have neglected the School, and if we add the two regna together we account for no less than 74 years of Stoneygate's history. As with Oliver there were various conflicts with the Council and several committees were set up to enquire into the unsatisfactory condition of the School. Whilst these committees could make recommendations and were given the power to act, nothing further ever appears to have been done, except tinkering with the position of the Usher (Assistant Master).

In the end the Mayor and the Council were probably glad to see Harris go in 1835 when he resigned through ill-health. In a history of the School which featured in a *Preston Herald* of 1894, the writer 'Battleaxe' assessed Harris' time as one of gradual decay, both in terms of reputation and the decline in the number of scholars. No boarders were taken after 1819 which was believed to have contributed to unruly behaviour through lack of pupil control out of school. Standards all round were poor, and to this could be added the dilapidated state of the buildings, some of which required urgent remedial work in 1831. But an even more fundamental problem was the site of the School, which had become an obstacle due to the deterioration of Stoneygate itself. As Preston had increased in size and prosperity the neighbourhood had lost its suburban character and become largely a manufacturing district, whereas at one time gentlemen's private residences had occupied the eastern side. Parents and pupils needed to be attracted again. The time had come for a radical rethink.

CROSS STREET,
THE JEWEL IN THE CROWN

On receiving Harris' resignation the Council appointed yet another committee to examine the conduct and management of the School, including subjects to be taught, what masters would be required and what their salaries and allowances should be. In addition the Headmaster's house would be more valuable for commercial purposes and the School, if rebuilt on a better site, might attract more pupils and therefore more fees. Standards needed to be vastly improved and the whole operation should be run on the same basis as a propriety school. Significantly when the Rev George Nun Smith was appointed as Headmaster it was on the condition that he held no competing post or permanent ecclesiastical duty (later relented upon). On the face of it the Council appeared to have retaken control, and even went so far as to state that it was willing to undertake the expense of rebuilding the School on a more appropriate site and scale.

At the beginning of 1836 new elective councils came into being with the passing of the 1835 Municipal Corporations Act. Inevitably a new committee was appointed and whilst it made the decision to return the Headmaster's house to a state fit for habitation – it became the *Arkwright Arms* – not a great deal else was done with regard to the proposed new premises. Smith in the meantime lived in Avenham House at his own expense.

The breakthrough came in 1841 when the Committee was authorised to consult with Smith. For the return of a small increase in pupils' fees he offered to fund a larger schoolroom on a plan and elevation to be agreed by the Treasurer. This was approved with the additional proviso that any monies obtained from the rent or sale of the old schoolhouse should go towards the new one. In the event the project was not financed by Smith alone but by a group of private shareholders who raised £2,550, and capital borrowed from Pedder's Bank. One would assume that most of the shareholders had or would have an interest in Winckley Square given the mutual benefits a new Grammar School would bring to the newly-developing area.

The site chosen was further down the course of the Syke from Stoneygate, at the bottom of the southern slope of Fishergate, on land that was principally garden ground. The building would front on to Cross Street, and its eastern boundary, later bordered by Guildhall Street, was part of a rear garden formerly owned by Bold Fleetwood-Hesketh, one-time High Sheriff of Lancashire, whose house was on Fishergate. The extensive garden and the house were separated by two lodges and a handsome gateway, but the whole would make way for the street in 1878.

With the site purchased from Ellen Cross, the architect John Welch was commissioned to design the School building. It would have to be conceived on a somewhat grandiose scale not only to make a statement to potential pupils but also to sit comfortably with the 'tone' of its nearby neighbour Winckley Square. This had been very deliberately set to the level of 'superior/fashionable' by William Cross on coming up with the idea of purchasing the Town End Field from Thomas Winckley and laying out plans for its residential development. There is no doubt that Cross had been seduced by the squares he had seen as a student in London, but he surely could not have failed to see what had and what was happening elsewhere in the heart of Preston, where the 'gentlemen' of Preston and the Grammar School were being overtaken by the same events.

Much of the land to the south of Fishergate and Church Street had been medieval fields and burgage plots, but the first part of the nineteenth century saw it being 'gobbled up' by the inward expansion of the industrialisation that was taking place. Socially this had generated an 'invasion' of the working classes in slum and cramped housing conditions, bringing with it poverty, pestilence and disease in a town already beset by a high mortality rate. This had affected the Grammar School in Stoneygate and the phenomenon was spreading quickly westwards, so from the moment that Cross built the first house in 1799, the continuing development of Winckley Square can be seen as a direct reaction, a sort of 'last stand' of the upper classes within the residential context of the town centre. Certainly by 1835 this spatial segregation had already become marked when a Report highlighted that the Christ Church Ward, which included Winckley Square, was top-heavy with 'gentlemen', millowners, lawyers and other professionals. Significantly, given the general health conditions of the town, these would later include doctors. By contrast the other wards were populated principally by working-class people (St Peters and Fishwick) and by shopkeepers and tradesmen (the market wards).

The lines thus drawn up in the urban landscape were not just about class, they were also about affluence, as well as business, communications and networking. Wealthy new millowners rubbed shoulders with professionals and leading citizens, and all had to comply with the rigid (and undoubtedly expensive) standards laid down by William Cross, and after his death in 1827, his widow Ellen. How would the new Grammar School meet this challenge?

Very quickly, if the unlikely but generally-held opening date of 1841 is to be believed. In fact Smith was only given the go-ahead by the Council in August of that year and an elaborately-decorated building constructed from Longridge stone could not have been completed in four months. Clearly the move must have taken place in 1842, a date supported by railway land purchase documents, one of which reports the event to the Lords Commissioners of the Treasury.

Notwithstanding, Welch rose ably to the visual aspect of the challenge with an edifice designed in the Tudor or Tudoresque style, incorporating a number of ornate and distinguishable features, not the least of which was the impressive arched entrance above four steps. This was surmounted by a panel which depicted a crowned Tudor Rose and a Portcullis with crown at either side of a shield bearing the Arms of Preston, the Paschal Lamb couchant, carrying a bannered cross above the letters PP. In addition in the upper left corner of the shield there was a compartment containing a hand holding a book, with the inscription 'Dignus es aperire' ('You are/be worthy to open' [the book/the seals]), whilst behind it were a

The School coat of arms with motto
From the front cover of a PGSA brochure. The motto translates as
'Long live the Queen, let the Church flourish, may the fortune of the House endure'
Preston Grammar School Association (PGSA)

mace and a crozier in saltire. The whole was surrounded by a ribbon with the words of the School motto 'Vivat Regina Floreat Ecclesia Stet Fortuna Domus' ('Long Live the Queen, Let the Church Flourish, May the Fortune of the House Endure'). There has been much speculation about the use of the word 'Regina' ('Queen') rather than 'Rex' ('King') in the motto, but there is no reason to believe that there was any bountiful Queen in the history of the School – it was no doubt purely a tribute to Victoria. The Tudor Rose to the left was the badge of the House of Tudor and the Portcullis to the right was the badge of the Beauforts from whom Henry VII was descended.

Interestingly it does not seem that the School ever had a formal grant of Arms, and in the twentieth century the Governors deemed it too expensive an act to pursue. Nevertheless it is generally assumed that the Arms adopted were of great antiquity. On the other hand it is not known whether they were present on earlier buildings, and in truth it has never been proven that they existed at all before Cross Street. Given the 'Regina' inscription and the sudden desire to identify with the powerful and propagandist Tudors it is highly likely that it was an exercise designed to establish the credentials of the School, set the architectural standards, attract a better (wealthier) class of pupil and maintain the ethos of Winckley Square. It was the means by which to reinvent history. Was the actual history, which went much further back than the Tudors, not known about, misunderstood or simply discarded in favour of being 'posh'? Notwithstanding, the panel was a fitting testament to the skills of Thomas Duckett, who later sculpted the statue of Sir Robert Peel in Winckley Square, and it is instantly recognisable to any Old Boy as its image adorned the front of all exercise books.

A stone gable above the panel contained a three-light mullioned window and the whole was flanked by two tall octagonal turrets, with latticed and glazed loopholes, topped with pointed (onion-shaped) domes protruding from crenellations, a very idiosyncratic touch from Welch. Running to the east was a wall containing an entrance into the yard, a stone gateway with carved roundels, which with a new wall later running north effectively formed the boundary of the School when Guildhall Street was laid out in 1878. This gateway was removed by the PGS Association in 1932 to serve as an entrance to the Grammar School building at the eastern end of Moor Park Avenue, where it remains today as an integral part of the Moor Park High School and Sixth Form.

Another building to the west of the main entrance was erected in 1845 and named the 'Collegiate Library'. It was used as a classroom for the senior boys and was decorated with stained glass designed by Thomas Willement and manufactured by Ballantynes of Edinburgh. This addition was financed by raising the fees of the senior boys by one guinea per annum.

In taking a walk inside the T-shaped building (the Cross Street entrance being the base of the 'T') there is probably no better way than being invited in by a relative contemporary. In 1857 Charles Hardwick wrote:

'. . . (it) contains on the ground floor a hall for recreation, sixty feet in length. The principal storey consists of a lofty open roofed hall for study, class room, and a transept, forty feet long. On the ground floor of the transept is the school-room, forty feet in length by twenty in width. The windows of the hall bear some resemblance to those of Merton College, Oxford. Adjoining, to the west, is the 'Collegiate Library', above which is a school room for the superior classes. The latter, which was originally intended for the reception of the books composing Dr Shepherd's Library, is decorated with some excellent specimens of stained glass by Ballantyne'.

He then goes on to describe the principal hall as being 'elaborately ornamented with pictures in distemper, painted by Frank Howard, representing subjects from English history, interspersed with decorative ornaments, mottoes etc.' In fact this description may have been the origin of a myth as the pictures were not painted in distemper on the wall.

The main building had three rooms with oak-coloured panelling and baronial-style fireplaces, the 'Greek', 'Latin' and 'English' 'schools'. Nothing is known of any Greek or Roman illustrations so these may never have happened. Hardwick is describing the 'English School' which had a large gable end devoted to subjects of English history. We are not certain of the finished state of the mural, but from a paper presented by the artist Frank Howard (1805–1866), and reproduced in two

Boys by the gate in Cross Street
Sepia postcard, PDA

versions by Richard Birtles in 1849, we can at least get an idea of his intentions. We can also get an idea that his services might not have come cheap although at the time he was described as earning a 'precarious livelihood' following a move from London to Liverpool. At any event he was a graduate of the Royal Academy, who later became something of a writer but who specialised in depicting scenes from history and literature (especially Shakespeare). He was the perfect choice for the ethos of the Cross Street building. Interestingly his pictures were sometimes referred to as 'cartoons'.

Howard had been commissioned by a patron of the School, John Addison, the Judge of the County Court and Recorder of Clitheroe, who had followed William Cross into 7 Winckley Square on the latter's move to Red Scar. His paper, presented to the Historical Society of Lancashire and Cheshire, interestingly confirms the intention of the Council and the shareholders to place the School on a footing with 'the best public schools in the kingdom.' He describes the School as 'fast rising into eminence', with the new and adjoining buildings forming 'a very picturesque composition'. His commission was an opportunity to make the walls 'a medium of instruction in history', no doubt to reinforce the School's standing in the scheme of things and to justify his own role.

The Cross Street gate today
This was removed from Cross Street to Moor Park Avenue in 1932.
Sara Park, Moor Park High School and Sixth Form (MPHSSF)

The large gable end of the English School was twenty-eight feet high above wainscot panelling and twenty-six feet wide. Whilst the finished product is described as a mural it was in fact a series of oil paintings on paper, which were pasted to canvas and then fastened on battens previously secured to the wall. The individual 'compartments' were crafted in Liverpool and transported to Preston, and Howard considered that his method afforded as much brilliance as fresco whilst combining the greatest durability with convenience of execution. They obviously took some time to complete as he describes them as 'now putting up'. It would also appear that pressure was put on Howard to depict local scenes and scenes from the history of Lancashire. Addison had been keen to attract other patrons to extend the decorations, but Howard claimed to have eschewed local scenes on the ground that he already had more than enough subjects to cover the history of England. There are later indications, however, that he may have backed down.

A lithograph of the wall, on the scale of half-an-inch to the foot, was produced to illustrate Howard's designs, but there are marked differences between this and his own description in the paper. At the apex of the gable according to Howard a single subject was planned, the 'Introduction of Christianity into the North of England', but the lithograph depicts the Battle of Hastings, 'The Introduction of a New Race'. Other disparities are clearly evident so modifications appear to have taken place at different times. In many cases the descriptions do not match. It was clearly an evolving project.

Below the apex of the gable the space to be decorated was divided into four horizontal rows, distinguished by 'arches of the four leading styles of architecture'. The upper series of three arches was semi-circular (Norman), the second of seven pointed (Lancet), the third of nine florid Gothic and the lowest of four Tudor. The subjects according to the lithograph (and not the description) were:

Apex
    The Battle of Hastings – The Introduction of a New Race

Norman
    Henry I founding Cambridge University (the introduction of learning)
    Henry II holding the stirrup of Thomas à Becket (abasement of Crown to Church)
    Henry II establishing the Flemish Weavers at Pembrokeshire (manufacturing)

Lancet
    Richard Coeur de Lion, with Philip of France, going to the Crusades (navy/ chivalry)
    Constance of Bretagne and Prince Arthur (dispossessed by King John)
    King John signing Magna Carta (recognition of popular rights)
    Froissart and Chaucer, exemplifying history and poetry (in allusion to the School)
    Henry III meeting his armed Parliament (second recognition of popular rights)
    Edward III and Philippa, founder of the Order of the Garter
    Edward the Black Prince leading his prisoner King John of France, into London (development of continental relations)

Florid
    Richard II and Watt Tyler (demonstration of democratic element in the Constitution)
    Richard II taught to read by his mother from an illuminated prayer book
    Richard II disguised as a monk (possibly)
    Margaret of Anjou, the representative of the Red Rose
    The Coronation of Henry VI

The lithograph depicting the paintings on the gable wall
Not seen for many years and the subject of much speculation.
Frank Howard (the author's collection)

Richard Neville, the king-making Earl of Warwick, representative of the
  White Rose
Edward IV and Elizabeth Woodville, the triumph of the White Rose (possibly)
The Children in the Tower
The Battle of Bosworth Field and the death of Richard III

Tudor

Henry VIII dismissing Cardinal Wolsey (the downfall of the Papacy)
Edward VI giving the Liturgy to Bishop Ridley (founding of English Church)
Armed men interrupting the reading of the Bible under Mary
Elizabeth holding Council for defence against the Armada (last Papacy
  attempt)

Many symbolic embellishments between the panels showing other links to
people and great historical events are listed by Howard, but apart from the carved
tabernacle work surmounting the florid Gothic arches, these features are difficult
to distinguish on the lithograph if they are portrayed at all. He did intend to include
the Scottish Lion on the extreme right of the gable wall, to allude to the Stuart
dynasty which would follow on the adjoining wall, but there is no further record of
this.

Due to the conflicting nature of Howard's and others' accounts there is a lot
of misinformation about this history of England mural, and to cloud the issue
the only known lithograph disappeared in the Harris Art Gallery many years ago.
Presumably the illustrated image is the same as the original but this is by no means
certain. It came from the Birtles book, sold at auction several years ago.

That the mural existed is not in doubt. In 1866 a report stated that the 'cartoons'
needed 'dusting' and the Council decided in 1892 that £20 should be spent on
renovating the 'pictures'. We have previously seen what 'cartoons' indicated. They
are described in 1900 by the Headmaster the Rev H. C. Brooks as interesting
reminders of the past. He does however add to the confusion by observing that 'the
characters introduced into the portions representing the reception of James I by the
Burgers of Preston display the features of several past masters and scholars of the
Grammar School', thereby indicating another set of modifications which incorporated at least one local scene, an idea formerly rejected. This may very well be the
end of the debate as no one knows exactly what actually happened to the pictures.
They would not have fitted in with the new building in Moor Park but it is difficult
to believe that they would have just been dumped. And the Council remained in
confusion right until the Cross Street building was being demolished in 1957. The
Curator of the Art Gallery, Sydney Paviere, was given the task of examining the
walls in the prevailing belief that the pictures had been painted on the gable wall
(presumably in distemper). Of course he found nothing. The destruction of the
School buildings was tragic enough, but where are the pictures?

Another interesting feature noted by Brooks in Cross Street was '*the* stained glass window', which was transferred to the Moor Park building. As a former pupil I always remember it being held in the deepest reverence and it was genuinely believed to be of Tudor origin. It certainly looked authentic. However Brooks himself did not describe it as being 'Tudor', and nor did anyone I consulted who attended the School in the 1930s, including the author of the *History*, the late Jim Heppell. It is likely that the belief grew from an article published in the School Magazine (*The Hoghtonian*) in 1940 by the Art Master, Henry (Harry) Ogle:

'The stained glass window of three lights . . . is an original work of the sixteenth century. Its period is Tudor, but it is for the expert in heraldry and glass painting to decide whether it was painted in the reign of Henry VIII, Edward VI or Queen Elizabeth.

(It) was designed as a complete royal armorial decoration: that is to say, a shield of arms surmounted by a crown and encircled by the Garter, and with supporters right and left.

. . . As a work of art the window is a first-rate example of its period, just when decadence both in heraldry and in glass painting began. The emblems and supporters admirably fill their appointed spaces, the drawing is vigorous and powerful, and the colour rich and varied . . . The brushwork and sparing use of fussy shading show artistic insight such as is seldom found today.'

Ogle gives a very detailed description of the window, and apart from one or two queries and discussions it remained 'Tudor' until there was talk of relocating it in 1973. The legend was that the window had come from Hampton Court Palace and that the arms were those of Henry VIII. This was certainly the belief in the late 1950s and 1960s. The value was estimated to be £500,000. However, on re-examining the window in 1975, Stephen Sartin, a fellow Old Boy and the then Assistant Keeper of Arts at the Harris Museum, discovered some anomalies, not the least of which included the fact that the shield did not display the normal Royal Arms, since the three lions were in profile and not facing the observer. He concluded that the window had been designed by Thomas Willement for Ballantyne and Allan of Edinburgh, the company responsible for putting all the other stained glass windows into the Cross Street building in 1845. It had also provided the windows for the new Houses of Parliament in the 1840s, and by coincidence had worked on Hampton Court and Preston Parish Church during the same period. Thus it is not difficult to see how the legend might have become 'fact'.

As late as 2009 Penny Hebgin-Barnes, having just compiled a catalogue of Medieval Stained Glass in Lancashire, wrote of her recent discovery of the window in the online magazine *Vidimus*, and adhered to the legend, citing the rich and

The 'Tudor' window
Removed from Cross Street to the Moor Park building in 1913.
Unlikely to be genuinely Tudor.
Sara Park, MPHSSF

expensive colours and the similarity of the heraldic panel to others believed to have been removed from Hampton Court. She concluded that Willement had probably taken the glass in part payment for his work at Hampton Court and reused it for Cross Street. There is also the question of why the Preston Coat of Arms is absent on a feature designed for Cross Street (it is present on the panel), but surely the real questions are what would Willement's motives have been and why was no one aware of the presence of a royal window? This in itself would have caused quite a stir and added even more legitimacy to the Tudor 'evidence'.

It is difficult to believe that the original glass painter of Hampton Court Palace, possibly Galyon Hone, would have made a basic error with the shield, but that would also be the case with an armorial expert such as Willement, unless of course it was a deliberate ploy to bypass ownership, a common practice amongst Victorian copyists and since. And of course reproduction is precisely what they excelled at, as evidenced by other parts of the Cross Street building and some of its contents.

The Headmaster's chair
A Victorian reproduction, not of Jacobean origin.
Photograph by the author

There are other problems with the window. Two of the lions in the bottom quarter are upside down and there are colour and design discrepancies which may or may not have arisen from poor renovation work, of which there are several examples. Stephen Sartin's research and findings certainly raised more than grave doubts on the antiquity of the window and alongside this we should readily acknowledge that the Victorians were superb fabricators with a particular penchant for colour vibrancy in stained glass. What is certain is that it is a very imposing and beautiful window and we know its exact location. It was removed from Cross Street to the new Moor Park Grammar School building in 1913, and remains there, opposite the old Headmaster's Study and to the right of the main entrance to the Moor Park High School and Sixth Form. With the intervention of the Grammar School

Association it never found its way to the then Tuson College or the Harris Museum and is rightly treasured and well cared for in its current location.

Having considered the architecture, design, layout and some of the decorations of the building in Cross Street, it would be interesting to look at what it contained by way of utilities and furniture. The truth is that not a lot is known. However, returning to Brooks and his 'interesting reminders of the past', he laments the fact that the old loose stalls or studies, at one time a distinguishing feature of the Sixth Form room in the Upper School, had vanished within quite recent times. But he takes comfort in drawing attention to the 'venerable oaken chair, with its curious carving'. This was in fact the 'Headmaster's Chair' (known as the 'President's Chair' by the Association), and there is a photograph taken around the turn of the twentieth century which features Brooks seated at the table in his study with the chair clearly visible in the background in front of the open door. The rest of the furniture is typical of its environment and is obviously of good quality, but the chair was special, and possibly not in a way that Brooks would have understood at the time.

The chair in the Headmaster's room, *c*.1900
It is clearly visible in the background in front of the open door.
The author's collection

The date of the chair is not known but it was always believed to have been of genuine Jacobean origin. There are several Tudor/Gothic features, including a huntsman back panel. At first glance it looks like the real thing. However, if we consider the need of the Cross Street School to establish its own historical links and credentials in order to make it more grandiose and attractive, and examine it again, we can see the same sort of anomalies that Sartin discovered with the stained glass window. It has features from different periods and is generally poorly constructed.

It was confirmed as not being 'right' by Maurice Barker, another Old Boy of the School and a former Crafts Master. It is a typical Victorian confection, a 'cobbling together' with which any buyer of such furniture is aware. It does have some quality and is made of oak, but the Jacobean patina has been created by the use of stain and not the effect of old age. It is nevertheless a very interesting piece which tells us a great deal about the 'vision' of the Cross Street School, and may offer us some clues as to the genuine 'antiquity' of the stained glass window and the Coat of Arms. It does not detract however from the fact that the School, through the physical manifestations of its Tudor-style propaganda, could seemingly and demonstrably trace its roots back to the fifteenth century. Interestingly the chair is not unique, as other examples (although less elaborate) exist in Buxton Museum and Art Gallery.

It is our good fortune that the chair is still around. It was removed in 1913 to the Moor Park building where it lived in the Headmaster's study, being used for ceremonial occasions, team photographs and as an aid to the art of caning, depending on who was Headmaster. It then spent many years at what is now

The School lectern

Norman Hodgson, Headmaster 1926–47, presumably posing by the lectern and not delivering the morning service, as R. C. Brown's organ is padlocked.

J. R. M. Heppell (PGSA)

Preston's College, before it was recovered by the Grammar School Association. Today it takes pride of place in the bay of the huge stained glass window in the hall of the old Grammar School, having been presented to the Moor Park High School and Sixth Form.

It is in the good company of the School lectern, which travelled exactly the same route from Cross Street via Preston's College. Constructed in a very solid fashion from oak, it bears a brass plaque which tells us that it was presented to the School to commemorate John Adams, a master there (Cross Street) from 1901 to 1906.

The School lectern today
Sara Park, MPHSSF

There is also an image from around the turn of the twentieth century depicting the staircase from the Shepherd room to the Sixth Form room and Chemical Laboratory. The balustrade is of decorative cast iron (Coalbrookdale?) with a wooden rail and the steps lead eventually to an entrance with what looks like a lancet arch. However, a testimony from G. W. Martin, Senior French Master, on his retirement in 1943, tells us that by 1907 when he joined the staff, the main building was no longer fit for purpose. There were three classes in the hall which made work difficult and there was no common room for the staff, although an underground playground was very useful on wet days. At the end of the hall was the stationery room where the Headmaster personally inspected old exercise books and doled out new ones, and where, incidentally, he kept his cane. The School had already been condemned by HM Inspectors in the person of a Mr McNaughton.

However, our main focus is on what the School brought to Winckley Square, and vice-versa. By 1842 the Square had not only attracted the 'gentlemen', the professionals and the wealthy, it could also lay claim to being the new cultural centre of Preston, which tied in perfectly with the presence of its now historically-distinguished Grammar School, a situation which also worked well in reverse. In 1841 the recently re-established Literary and Philosophical Society merged with the Preston Society of Arts, acquiring along the way a collection of works of art and a library of books. Many of the great and good of Winckley Square had been in one or both of these societies, and the task of the combined committees was now to find more suitable premises for their activities and artefacts. At the same time the 'Gentlemen's Coffee Room', a rather exclusive social club, was looking to move from Lancaster Road, so the two groups combined forces to purchase from Ellen Cross adjoining plots of land which cornered on the east side of Winckley Square and the north-west side of Cross Street, where one abutted the Grammar School. John Welch was commissioned to design and build the new structures which both opened in 1846. The social club, renamed the Winckley Club, occupied the plot on Winckley Square and the Literary and Philosophical Society shared Cross Street with the Grammar School, a most appropriate and mutually convenient arrangement.

The new architectural cluster was outstanding even by the standards of Winckley Square. In Mannex's 1851 Trade Directory there is no mention of the growing number of desirable houses bordering the Square yet attention is explicitly drawn to the 'splendid range of Tudor-style buildings' situated at the junction of Winckley Square and Cross Street. They are noted as housing the Literary and Philosophical Institution, a long-established competitor of the Institute for the Diffusion of Knowledge; the exclusive Winckley Club, with its news and billiard rooms; and the Grammar School, giving fee-paying boys a classical education. Hardwick refers to them as 'one of the chief architectural ornaments of the town', and the general consensus appeared to be that the Grammar School was the most magnificent of structures, the jewel in the crown, a view sadly not held a century later.

By 1859 temporary repairs were required on the School buildings, but the shareholders were evidently unwilling to pay for it. In early 1860 Philip Park and I. B. Dickson offered the School to the Council for sale or rent. Further negotiations resulted in the Council purchasing it for £1,347 10s 0d (the figure quoted in

The Cross Street staircase, c. 1900
The author's collection

the Minutes), an amount that included £350 plus interest still owing to Pedders Bank. At the same time £68 was laid out for a heating system and the installation of gas lighting.

1866 was a successful year for the School, which was rapidly outgrowing its facilities. By now the Literary and Philosophical Society had been in decline for some years and the Council made the decision to purchase its buildings and contents for the sum of £1,527 10s 0d a year later. What happened next has been subject to some debate. Marian Roberts states unequivocally that the building was used to house Dr Shepherd's books and that it came to be known as 'Dr Shepherd's Library and Museum'. In 1883 Hewitson had said something very similar, mentioning that it contained the manuscripts of the *History of Lancashire* by Edward Baines (who had finished his education at Preston Grammar School) and describing an oil painting of Dr Shepherd at one end of the library room, which was adjoined by a reading room. A few years later Brooks added that the Library (had) overlooked Winckley Square, remarking in an almost proprietary way that when in Shepherd Street it

The 'cluster' of buildings, *c.* 1850
An engraving depicting (left to right) the Winckley Club,
the Literary and Philosophical Society, and the Grammar School.

PDA

had likewise been a neighbour of the Stoneygate Grammar School. Heppell on the other hand states that the building was never employed to house the Library and in his 1857 report Hardwick claimed that it was already in use by the School. Both may have confused it with the Collegiate Library, which had at one time been earmarked for Dr Shepherd's collection and was part of the main School.

What is clear is that the contents of the Library were transferred to the recently-opened Harris Museum in 1895 and that following a refurbishment and reopening of the School in 1898, 'the building adjoining the Grammar School . . . came into use as part of the School premises' (Brooks' 1900 Prospectus). It is likely that the Shepherd Room alluded to earlier was also in that building as plans for the equipment of 'Chemical and Physical Laboratories' were soon to be carried into effect, and the staircase in the image led to the 'Chemical Laboratory' (the facilities of the Harris Institute being used hitherto). At the same time the School in general benefitted from, amongst other things, a new dinner room, a lavatory, a cloakroom, a new entrance from the outdoor playground to the covered playground and improvements to the covered playground which incorporated provision for storing bicycles. 'Physical drill' and swimming were added to a new curriculum and the Library Committee approved the 'loans of pictures for hanging upon the walls and of books of reference for the use of the boys' (Brooks). At this point the Grammar School physically arrived in Winckley Square.

Notwithstanding, as an integral part of the cluster of buildings it had always had a spiritual presence, and returning to earlier years it prospered, at least initially. By 1854 pupil numbers had gone up to 115, of which ten were the sons of freemen. However, the cost of running the School exceeded the income from the Worthington land and it effectively lost its status as a free School. Two years later the sons of non-freemen were included in the ten places nominated by the Council but this was not permanently adhered to. A snapshot of the time shows the subjects taught to be Scripture, Greek, Latin, Modern Languages, Geography, Chemistry, the Histories of Rome and England, Mathematics and Mechanical Drawing, providing a truly classical education. The first record of a prize-giving ceremony was in 1857, being held annually thereafter, with the prizes being given by the Mayor in full regalia, accompanied by members of the Council and the Examiner, a Mr E. G. Hancock, Fellow of St John's College, Cambridge. The School Captain was Miles Myres, later Vicar of St Paul's Church, Preston, and father of Sir John Linton Myres. The Myres family will be discussed later.

With a new Headmaster in 1857, the Rev John Richard Blakiston, the Council determined to increase the catchment area for pupils and to specifically prepare boys for the Universities, the Army and the Navy. Boarders would be taken, the Upper School staying in the Headmaster's house and the Lower School in the Second Master's house. By 1864 it had also been realised that many boys were starting school late or arriving unschooled and it was decided to introduce a Preparatory School, which was so successful that in 1869 it had to expand from Avenham House to the lower rooms of the main School. Some, such as the future Lt-Gen Sir Percy Henry Noel Lake, attended the Prep School to prepare themselves for Public School, in his case Uppingham.

From 1864 boys began to take part in civil events on a regular basis where they would mingle with the great and the good, including no doubt many residents of Winckley Square. Achievements began to be recorded on wooden tablets, and in 1871 a limited scholarship scheme based on examination results was introduced. Later, in 1911 whilst still in Cross Street, a House system was adopted, the Houses being named after the benefactors Goodair, Harris, Miller and Thornley. But it was also whilst at Cross Street that the death knell for the School had possibly sounded. We have already seen how it had lost its charitable status, but with a change in the law of secondary education the Council in 1904 took over the running of the School, receiving a grant from but being under the control of the Board of Education. This placed it in the same position as all other secondary schools, which meant that it would benefit from improvements but would lose any independence it might have had.

The Grammar School and Winckley Square were good for each other, but it was not all plain sailing. Money was always an issue, and in many ways the wellbeing of the School reflected that of Stoneygate in that it depended on the goodwill and

Alfred Beaven Beaven and the Rev Henry Brooks
Two contrasting Headmasters.
The Old Boy's Magazine *1913* (*PGSA*)

commitment of the Headmaster. We have seen how it prospered in the early years of Cross Street under the Rev George Nun Smith (1835–55) but after his resignation and a short tenure by his brother Edwin Smith (1855–57) pupil numbers declined again. When the Rev George Turner Tatham arrived at the School in 1859 he found it in a sorry state with only 19 pupils, but numbers increased under his Headmastership to a maximum of 158 in 1873. Of course other factors sometimes came into play. Numbers decreased temporarily in 1863 on account of depressed world economic conditions and the American Civil War, both of which resulted in a cotton famine. There had also been the previous 'Lock Out' of 1853/54. The closure of cotton mills affected the whole of Preston's economy and this would be keenly felt in Winckley Square.

The next Headmaster Alfred Beaven Beaven (1874–98) was something of a disaster. His reign did not get off to a good start. The boys had to wait five years for adequate toilets to be built and in 1878 a bitter dispute arose around the dumping of spoil on the School yard as Guildhall Street was being laid out. This was only settled with the threat of legal action. One of his first acts was to introduce the three-term School year and there is no doubt he was an excellent academic but he was an exacting and fearsome man with a nasty side to him. He was taken to court in 1877 for assault when he caned William Paley, a member of the cotton family, but this was normal for him and the punishment was deemed not to be excessive. In 1882 he started a bitter feud with Louisa Frances Walsh, Headmistress of Preston High School for Girls (overlooking Winckley Square), during the course of which he consistently questioned her credentials and her character. A very public spat led her to resign a year later. Other examples of his spitefulness abound, some of which will be detailed in the later descriptions of School luminaries. He was also perpetually in debt, a problem that would eventually come to haunt him. But despite all this the School examination results were exemplary. The problem was that the number of scholars dwindled from 137 in 1882 to 32 in 1898, which was seen to be directly attributable to his methods. A combination of pressure from the Council and competition from the Harris Institute offering commercial subjects forced his resignation without financial settlement in 1898 and that was the end of Beaven Beaven.

It would be no overstatement to claim that the Rev Henry Cribb Brooks (1898–1911) arrived to save the School. Faced with the fact that Beaven Beaven had left no records he introduced a programme of reform with the Council which addressed the practical needs (including financial) as well as the academic ones. The furniture was repaired but mats and decent washing facilities were required and he started a Physics laboratory, for the time being leaving the Chemistry with the Harris Institute. He arranged free swimming for the boys at the Public Baths, published a brochure outlining a brief history of the School, introduced the Founder's Prayer and established new scholarships. Thus he was able to produce a credible prospectus in 1901 and the effect of his reforms was such that by 1902 the number of pupils had increased to 156. Despite the 1904 change in the law of secondary education, the condemnation of the School buildings by the HM Inspectorate from 1906 and the subsequent financial and political battles over the building of a new School, there were still 155 pupils in 1909, of whom 62 held scholarships. In just 13 years Brooks oversaw a complete reversal of fortunes, a remarkable achievement given the unsuitability of the building. The Grammar School would leave Winckley Square with head held high and many former pupils would be forever grateful.

CROSS STREET AND ITS PEOPLE

Preston Grammar School had an active presence of just over seventy years in Winckley Square. Who in this time passed through its doors and who were some of the people associated with it?

The Benefactors

It is fitting to begin with the benefactors. Brooks in 1900 listed Helen de Hoghton, Edward VI and Bartholomew Worthington, whom we encountered earlier. He went on to include Thomas Miller, Edmund Robert Harris, John Goodair, Edmund Thornley and William Henry Goodair, whose names later lent themselves to the School Houses, and added (but didn't name) the Mayors of Preston who had annually provided money for the purchase of the School prizes. He also outlined how in 1865 several small municipal charities connected with George Rogerson (1619), Henry Banester (1642), Thomas Winckley (1720) and Henry and Eleanor Rishton (1738) had lapsed for want of applicants and were consolidated to provide minor scholarships for the Grammar School.

The connection with Goodair went back to 1861, when John Goodair, not apparently an Old Boy, spotted that there was no financial assistance for scholars to attend university. He was a member of the Town Council who had made his money from cotton and he gave £200 towards a university exhibition. This was however not adequate in itself and in 1879 his son, Col William Henry Goodair, on his retirement from the mayoralty, added another £200. The interest on the total sum was allowed to accrue until £1,000 became available to introduce the Goodair Exhibition in 1904.

Thomas Miller was another cotton magnate, a self-made man who worked his way to the top with the firm of Horrockses Miller & Co and who became Mayor of Preston and an Alderman. He would not only be familiar with the Grammar School through his Council work, he lived just round the corner in Winckley Square in a house that would later become part of the Park School, the Girls' Grammar School. Miller of course presented the Park bearing his name to the Town in 1864, but he died at an early age a year later. In 1867 the Corporation established the Miller Exhibition which provided £40 annually from his bequest.

Local solicitor and former Prothonotary for Lancashire, Edmund Robert Harris, the last of his line, was one of the great benefactors of Preston. With his death in 1877 he left a massive legacy, much of it possibly from railway shares, which was largely devoted to religious, educational and philanthropic causes. The trustees of his estate ensured that the Free Library, Art Gallery and Museum, the Orphanage and the Institute and Technical College all came about, and £3,000 was given to the Grammar School via the Corporation for the foundation of scholarships. He had obviously not forgotten his upbringing and early life in Arkwright House, which extended over thirty years up until his father Robert resigning the Headmastership in 1835 and the family relocating to Ribblesdale Place. In the event two scholarships were established, both tenable at either Oxford or Cambridge.

The fourth name associated with the House system was another self-made local man, Edmund Thornley, a grocer and wine merchant who lived in Latham Street. In his will, proved in 1878, he left money to provide five smaller scholarships tenable at the School. These were later merged with the Miller and Goodair Exhibitions as the provision of free places made them unnecessary. Prior to them an Exhibition had been founded in 1865 by Thomas Winckley and the Walton Scholarships were established later in 1906. In addition there was a list of sponsors for the various School prizes.

This trend, established in Cross Street, later gathered such momentum that the Headmaster in 1952 was able to declare that the School was one of the best endowed Grammar Schools in the country, with a scholarship fund totalling £24,000 producing an annual income of £800. Of particular interest to us is the Fred Mayor Scholarship of that year. By living a very frugal life Fred Mayor's mother, following her death at the age of 91, was able to leave £2,500 to the School in memory of her son, who, despite his disadvantaged background won a scholarship to Cross Street and went on to University, finally becoming Headmaster at Hull Grammar School. Similarly the William Fawell Ascroft prize was established in memory of his grandfather who had attended Stoneygate and his father who had been at Cross Street from 1852. Clearly the Cross Street School had left an indelible mark.

Head Boys

Fred Mayor is a good example of a pupil doing well on a scholarship and progressing to the summit of his chosen career. There were many others who similarly passed through the School practically unnoticed but nevertheless went on to make light of their disadvantages. This was the major benefit of the scholarship system although of course money still talked. At a more noticeable level a cursory glance at some of the early School Captains/Head Boys gives us a clear indication of who might go on to do well. For example, James Taylor Brown (1845–49) was later appointed Vicar of Holy Trinity, Preston and Walter Lowe Clay became Vicar of Rainhill, along the way gaining a reputation as 'a very prominent clergyman of the 'Broad' Church school' (Hewitson). He was a son and the biographer of the Rev John Clay, Chaplain to Preston Gaol, a well-known prison reformer of his day and patron of Preston Grammar School. His brother was the artist Alfred Borron Clay (1831–1868) who also attended the Grammar School and whose portrait of Thomas Batty Addison

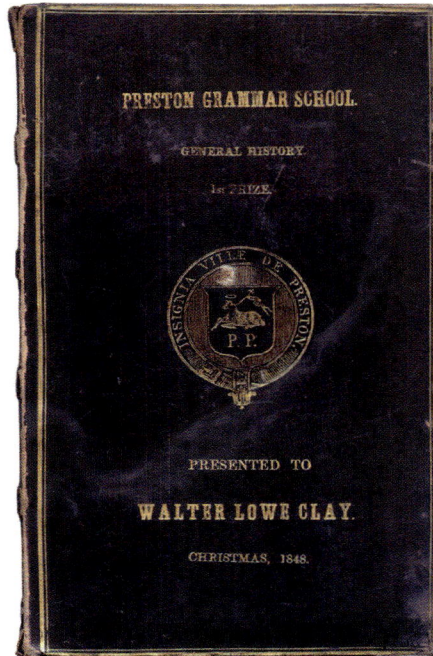

The oldest known School prize
Photograph by the author

still adorns the Preston Crown Courthouse. Interestingly the Grammar School Association had in its possession a book inscribed and presented to Walter Lowe Clay as First Prize in General History, Christmas 1848. It is unusual in that the insignia (a corporate one) and the inscription are embossed in gold on the front outer cover and that the prize was awarded nine years before official prize-giving commenced. It is the oldest known School prize and is now with the Moor Park High School and Sixth Form having initially been rediscovered during a house renovation in Derby where it had lain hidden in an attic for years. It's a strange old world.

John Eldon Gorst

John Eldon Gorst was School Captain for 1852–53. He lived his early years in Winckley Square before going on to Cambridge University and later arriving in New Zealand. Becoming involved in Maori affairs he was appointed Inspector of Native and Missionary Schools in Waikito in 1861 and a year later he became Civil Commissioner and a newspaper editor there, but with the Maori uprising he and his family had to make a hasty return to England. He was called to the Bar in 1865, becoming a Queen's Counsel in 1875. In 1866 he was elected Tory MP for Cambridge but lost his seat two years later. For the next few years he reorganised the Party machinery at the behest of Disraeli which paved the way for success at the 1874 elections and his own subsequent success in a by-election to represent Chatham in 1875. He was never a member of the Cabinet but he held many top government positions until 1902, at which time he was the Vice-President of the Committee of the Privy Council on Education. Whilst Solicitor-General in 1885 he was knighted, but later left the Tories, standing as an Independent in 1906 and a Liberal (for Preston) in 1910. He was unsuccessful on both occasions, but Sir John Eldon Gorst QC and former MP hadn't done badly out of Cross Street.

John Edmund Wentworth Addison

Gorst's successor as School captain was John Edmund Wentworth Addison. He was born in Bruges, Belgium, and was therefore no relation to the Addisons of Winckley Square. In many respects his career mirrored that of Gorst in that he went to University (Trinity College Dublin), was called to the Bar in 1862 (sooner than Gorst) and became a Queen's Counsel in 1880 (later). From 1874 to 1890 he was Recorder for Preston, by coincidence succeeding Thomas Batty Addison, and during this time he, like Gorst, embarked on a political career, entering Parliament as Tory MP for Ashton-under-Lyne in 1885. Re-elected the following year on the casting vote of the Returning Officer, he held his seat until 1895 before standing down. He resumed his legal career in the East Anglia area, having left Preston.

During the Guild Speeches of 1882, as Recorder, Addison gave the reply to the Headmaster, expressing his pleasure at the continued success of the School, adding that 'it shows no sign of decay; on the contrary . . . it lives, flourishes and grows'. He recalled the time in 1854 when he had addressed the Mayor in Latin, and after a laudatory allusion to the 'famous John Gorst', whom he had succeeded as Captain 'but never equalled', he urged the Head Boy to be encouraged by the results of hard work and to strive in turn to do some good, for 'you have entered upon a noble inheritance, and enjoy greater advantages than former generations'. Stirring words indeed from an Old Boy, who was later to repeat his performance as Chairman at the very first Dinner/Meeting of the Old Boys' Association at the Park Hotel in 1888.

The Myres Family

Addison was followed in 1855 by William Miles Myres, who became Vicar of St Paul's Church, Preston, and later Vicar of Swanbourne. His son, John Linton Myres, also attended the Cross Street School in 1879 before gaining a scholarship to Winchester and subsequent entrance to New College, Oxford, where he obtained outstanding results. He carried out archaeological work in the Eastern Mediterranean, lectured in Classical Archaeology at Oxford, was appointed Professor of Greek at Liverpool University and finally returned to Oxford as Wykeham Professor from where he retired in 1947. But he had a much more exciting life than this would give to expect!

In his unpublished memoirs John Linton reminds us that his uncles as well as his father attended Cross Street and that the Myres boasted two Mayors of Preston in the nineteenth century, meaning that several of the family were Guild Burgesses, another inextricable link between the School and the Town which continues today. He was proud to state that his father Miles as Head Boy had greeted the Mayor with a speech in Latin at the annual prize day, and that this had been reproduced in the *Preston Herald*. He recalled that Preston Grammar School, in common with other Grammar Schools still had memories of a Victorian 'barring out' and the subsequent siege of the School buildings (from which the pupils eventually escaped and managed to avoid punishment). He also gives a brief description of the inside of the School. In his day the Sixth and Fifth forms had separate studies opening through a gothic screen onto the classrooms where the Fourth and Third forms were taught. The larger lower forms occupied the great schoolroom, with open timber roof and painted canvas scenes from English history. However, in his view these canvases were too gloomy for further study apart from Queen Elizabeth who came down low over the fireplace, but they were 'well-placed for practice with darts made from pen holders'. So much for the idea of a painted distemper gable wall or the 'frescoes' described by William Pollard in 1882. Darts don't stick into plaster!

He adds that on the floor they had their own desks, 'much carved and slashed, and black with ink' and he describes the French teacher Mr Osborne as being 'volatile and master of the cane'. There was no regular playground except a basement under the great schoolroom and a small back yard. No games were allowed in Cross Street, and the whole was presided over by the infamous Alfred Beaven Beaven who was 'a good friend to those who would obey his instructions', but horribly cruel to any boy who aroused his interest. John Linton was unfortunately one and he sets the scene for the punishment: 'With immense black beard and flashing eyes and teeth, he would descend on Class or desks, hoist his victim over his shoulder and slash him with the black or the white ivory paperknife, which he sharpened on one or the other between attacks as he rushed up and down the School . . .'.

Sir Charles Holmes, prolific painter, art historian and Director of the National Gallery, was a boarder the year after John Linton (1880), and in his 1936 autobiography states that 'With his dark beard, beetling brow, eyeglass screwed tight into his right eye, and his reputation for flogging, Mr Beaven was a memorable figure as he poised himself two yards back from the lectern, and turned the doings of Elijah and Ahab into dramatic reality'. As noted earlier, Beaven Beaven got good examination results but only had about a dozen pupils left (according to Myres) before Brooks entered onto the scene and the School regained its earlier distinction. Cross Street had certainly been a memorable experience for Myres and Holmes.

It could actually be argued that John Linton Myres learned a few things from Beaven Beaven, for it was he who earned the nickname 'Blackbeard of the Aegean.' During the Great War he was a naval Lieutenant-Commander sent to the Aegean on account of his good knowledge of Greek and the geography of the area. He gathered a gang of Greek ruffians on his ship the tug *Syra* (and later the former Royal Yacht *Aulis*) and led expeditions to the west coast of Turkey, specialising in cattle raids. With a large black beard he reputedly resembled an Assyrian king with a touch of Blackbeard Teach, according to his colleague Compton Mackenzie.

Both Miles and John Linton Myres donated annual School prizes, and the latter took an interest in the School right up until his death in 1954, being Vice-President of the Association for many years. Yet another Old Boy from Cross Street, Sir John Linton Myres OBE MA FSA had done well whilst still remaining proud of his School background. In 2010 his grandson Rear-Admiral J. A. L. (John) Myres attended the Association Annual Dinner as Guest Speaker, where he reminded everyone with a glint in his eye that as a Burgess he attended Preston Guilds and that in 1972 as Commander of HMS *Fox* he had provided his own transport. Some entrance!

Percy Henry Noel Lake

Staying with the military theme, Sir Percy Henry Noel Lake KCB had attended Cross Street in the 1860s before going on to Uppingham. In 1873 he joined the 59th Foot (later the Second Battalion East Lancashire Regiment), serving with distinction on the North-West Frontier of India and in the Sudan. After a time spent in Canada and promotion to Lieutenant-General in 1911, he was sent back to India and appointed Chief of General Staff a year later. In 1915 in the ill-fated attempt to capture Baghdad Kut-el-Amara was besieged and on a second attempt Lake failed to lift the siege, with the inevitable consequence of bloodshed when Kut fell to the enemy. As he prepared for a new campaign he was summoned back to England to give evidence to the Mesopotamia Committee and he then worked in the Ministry of Munitions, retiring from the Army in 1919. He had been unlucky to get a difficult command so late into a brilliant career, although his successor General Maude testified to the excellent groundwork he had put in for the later campaign to succeed. Like John Linton Myres he was a long-standing Vice-President of the Association right up until his death in 1940 at the age of 85.

Herbert George Ponting

Arthur Winter, the well-known local photographer, was an Old Boy of Cross Street, but in keeping with other adventurers from the School Herbert George Pointing had a more remarkable career. His father Francis was a successful banker and his career took him, Herbert and the rest of the family to various parts of the country. In the 1880s, in between Carlisle Grammar School and Wellington House College, Leyland, Herbert found himself at Cross Street, although we know little of his time at the School, possibly on account of Beaven Beaven's failure to keep records and a lack of information in the Ponting archives. In 1888 he followed his father

Herbert George Ponting
In Antarctica with the Scott Polar Expedition of 1912.
en.wikipedia.org

into banking, but disgruntled he emigrated to California where he invested in gold mining and bought a fruit ranch. He married the socially well-connected Mary Biddle Elliott in 1895 and they had two children, Mildred and Arthur. However, his business ventures failed and he developed a passionate interest in photography, quickly getting noticed as someone who used the camera as a medium of art rather than a mere recorder of events and people. He travelled the world and as the techniques of printing improved his work began to be published in London's magazines, often alongside the Sherlock Holmes stories of Arthur Conan Doyle. In 1905 he became a Fellow of the Royal Geographical Society and his burgeoning career led to him deserting his family a year later.

With the publication of *In Lotus Land Japan* in 1910 his international reputation as a photographer and travel writer was confirmed and he was signed up by Robert Falcon Scott as photographer ('camera artist') for the Antarctic Expedition on the *Terra Nova*. He had mixed experiences, not always being a popular member of the party, almost being killed by a whale, excelling himself with a time-lapse sequence of a penguin egg hatching and being responsible for the introduction of a new word, 'pont', which meant to hold a pose, sometimes in an uncomfortable position and generally in the freezing cold (and he was a perfectionist!). In the event Scott did not take him to the true South Pole in 1912, which of course saved his life. On his eventual return to civilisation Ponting was not popular with the public, but this changed with the publication of *The Great White South* in 1921, and three years later he produced the film *The Great White Silence*, which, with graphics and reconstructions, was a stunning record of the expedition. With sound it was reworked as *90° South* and he received the Polar Medal, the Royal Geographical Society Medal and a medal from the Emperor of Japan. As ever, his ventures failed, he never did see his family again and he died in 1935. Still, an Old Boy of Cross Street is at least commemorated by Ponting Cliff in Northern Victoria Land, and as a postscript the grandfather of a Past President of the Association was first mate on the *Terra Nova* and knew Ponting.

Robert Charles Brown

In 1864 Henry Oldfield Pilkington was Head Boy, and he eventually became the Medical Officer of Health for Preston. Medicine was quickly becoming a professional option and one of Winckley Square's most famous residents, Dr Robert Charles Brown started out at the Cross Street Grammar School, attending there between 1845 and 1853. We have noted that his older brother, James Taylor Brown, was Head Boy at this time. In his fascinating book *Sixty-Four Years A Doctor* he recalls the time spent as House Surgeon to the old Preston Dispensary and from 1870 as a member of staff at the Preston Royal Infirmary, where the Brown Ward was later named after him. Aside from being the Medical Officer of Health for Preston he was also the Local Medical Officer to the London and North Western and the Lancashire and Yorkshire Railways, and some of his stories of medical procedures prior to the opening of the Infirmary make for grim reading. He did a lot to improve the health of the Town and he often funded new equipment for the Infirmary, including an operating theatre at a cost of £2,700. He looked after his nursing staff, and his outstanding medical career and thoughtful generosity were recognised by him being made an Honorary Freeman of the Borough in 1910 and later being awarded a knighthood.

Charles Brown was a very revered man in Preston. It is rather less well-known that he was a musician who loved to play the organ. For five years he was the organist at Holy Trinity Church, Preston, where his brother, the aforementioned Rev James

Robert Charles Brown
The 'grand old man' of Preston.
Sixty-Four Years a Doctor (*the author's collection*)

Taylor Brown was vicar from 1867 until his early death in 1875. He regularly played on Sundays at the Royal Infirmary where he had donated the instrument. He also donated organs to the Harris Orphanage and the Home for the Blind but the one that gave him the most satisfaction was the one built by Henry Ainscough of North Road for the new Grammar School building in Moor Park Avenue. He recorded 'It was one of the great pleasures of my life to give an organ to the Preston Grammar School, where I received the whole of my education, except the medical portion of it'. The inscription on the organ read: 'This Organ was presented by Robert Charles Brown, Esq., M.A. (Cantab). (Hon Cansa). F.R.C.P. (Lond). M.B. (Lond). F.R.C.S. (Eng)., Honorary Freeman of the Borough, an old boy of this School; and was opened on the 2nd. October, 1913, his 77th, birthday.' By his own admission he owed a great deal to his Grammar School education and as well as promoting the interests of organ music he had always sought to repay the debt.

The School organ with lectern, 1914
Rebecca Major (PGSA)

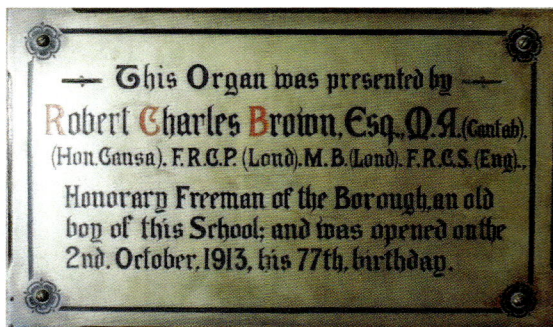

The organ inscription
Stephen Sartin (PGSA)

All Old Boys will remember the fine instrument well. It had three manuals, a pedal board, 18 speaking stops, six couplers and an electric blower and accompanied the hymn singing every morning at Assembly. It was quite able to sustain a full concert repertoire. As late as 1967 (two years before the School officially closed) the renowned organist Harry Gabb gave a recital consisting of a variety of short pieces that fully highlighted its capabilties. Sadly neglected it was dismantled in 1988 and no one is quite sure what happened to the parts if not rebuilt. Given the quality of the pipes one would assume they would have been reused to upgrade other instruments as Ainscough organs had and have a good reputation. There was a rumour that it had ended up reconstructed in Yorkshire, possibly Huddersfield, but there is no doubt the dismantlers were from Lancaster. Possibly the best example of an Ainscough organ is in Lancaster Cathedral but there is no record there of any major work in the late 1980s, the latest rebuild having been carried out by Henry Willis and Sons in 2007. One wonders what Sir Robert Charles Brown, Preston's 'Grand Old Man' and President of the Grammar School Association for no less than thirteen years, would have thought of this?

Percy George Coles

Earlier, the Senior French Master, D. G. Martin, was mentioned for stating on his retirement in 1943 that the Cross Street building had already been unfit for purpose when he joined the School in 1907. There was no hint of this from Percy George Coles who had become a member of staff (Mathematics) two years previously. In common with many mathematicians P. G. (known affectionately as 'Piggy') Coles was also a very skilled musician and when the move to Moor Park came in 1913 he was appointed as the only permanent titular organist in the history of the School if we discount the named pupil-organists. He obviously loved the Ainscough instrument presented by Brown and immediately drew up a specification for it. He also established the School Orchestra which was to survive until the closure of the School but was never remunerated for his music duties as he was already on the staff as a Maths teacher and Second Master. He retired in 1937 and passed away in 1945, with pupil-organist and former Preston North End Chairman Alan Jones playing at his funeral in Christ Church Fulwood. The fascinating thing about Martin and Coles is that there are Old Boys alive today who were taught by one or both of them and remember them well. The link to Cross Street (and by definition Winckley Square) is yet to be broken!

Samuel Leach

Going back a little in time, Samuel Leach, whose family lived at 5 Camden Place overlooking Winckley Square, moved in 1837 at the age of eight from a mixed school in Charles Street to the Grammar School in Stoneygate. In 1842 he transferred to the 'fine new buildings' in Cross Street from where he was able to make use of the Literary and Philosophical Society library at lunchtimes on account of his family having tickets to admit them all to the privileges connected with the Society. He would spend his evenings learning Latin and Greek by heart under gaslight, and

The Grammar School staff in 1905

P. G. Coles is second from the left, back row. The Headmaster, H. C. Brooks is second from the left, front row, whilst next to him, second from the right, is John Adams, to whom the lectern was dedicated.

PGSA (original now in the Lancashire Archives)

amongst his friends were James (Taylor) Brown, brother of Robert Charles, and John Rofe, son of the Gas Engineer, which allowed them to play in and around and very often on, the gasometers. At the age of eight he had the privilege of seeing the first ever train depart from Preston on the North Union line to Wigan.

On leaving School in 1845 Samuel decided to go into business with his brother John in Manchester rather than go to university, and five years later he joined his other brother, Joseph, a cotton broker in Liverpool, soon becoming a partner in the business. This followed in the tradition of his father Thomas, who held several directorships and distinguished positions in Preston companies, and who was a Town Councillor for a number of years, apparently rejecting the offer of the mayoralty. Like Robert Charles Brown, Samuel lived to a ripe old age (94), having written his autobiography seven years earlier.

The Harris Free Library, 1893
Looking extremely isolated on its completion.
PDA

James Hibbert

Whilst walking across Preston Flag Market no one can fail to be impressed by the front elevation of the Harris Museum, Library and Art Gallery. For this a debt is owed not only to the benefactor Edmund Robert Harris but also to the architect James Hibbert, another Old Boy of the Cross Street Grammar School. He, like many others, rose from humble beginnings to forge a successful career, and apart from excelling in his profession he was also elected Mayor in 1880.

In his early career he designed the Fishergate Baptist Church (1858) in partnership with Nathan Rainford, and went on to add amongst other things St Saviour's Church (1866), an extension to Preston Royal Infirmary (1866–70), Preston Savings Bank (1872), St Matthew's Church (1883) and a partial rebuild of the North Road

Pentecostal Church (1885–86) before his 'pièce de résistance', the Harris Museum, Library and Art Gallery, opened in 1893.

At a time when museum industrial collections were becoming important, it appears that Hibbert was making a stand against it, opting instead for Hellenistic values of liberal knowledge and humanism rather than materialism and commerce. It clearly bucked the trend, but Hibbert was in a powerful position. The responsibility for carrying out Edmund Harris' wishes was already delegated by the Corporation to a committee chaired by James Hibbert, simultaneously Chairman of the Free Library Committee and designated architect of the new building. Whilst such a degree of authority would today sit uncomfortably with accountability, it left Hibbert in almost complete control. Further, he had been elected to the Council in 1871, and as the best debater in the Chamber and having expert knowledge of the history of art, he was also intellectually and politically well-positioned to orchestrate the development, and he made no secret of his plans. He declared as early as 1881 that the aim was to provide a 'comprehensive permanent foundation for the encouragement of Learning, the cultivation of the Arts and Sciences and the free diffusion of a varied Literature', and this is what he did. The neo-classical design with the sculptures of Roscoe Mullins announced the purpose and plan of the interior. It was certainly markedly different from the Gothic Revival Town Hall of George Gilbert Scott and it was set slightly away from it on the eastern side of the market square. Perhaps it was controversial in its day but it has certainly stood the test of time, as will the modern Brutalist-style bus station.

Richard Corless

The above has been a brief snapshot of some of the better-known boys of the Cross Street Grammar School, but it would be remiss to omit Richard Corless whose large collection of beautifully bound, tooled and inscribed School prize books was in the possession of the Association until a recent transfer to the Moor Park High School and Sixth Form. These books were a true statement of class. Born in 1885 Richard was the bright boy of a family of eight children from Goosnargh, and from the village school he passed his scholarship and entered the Grammar School in 1896, at a time when only fifty pupils remained under Beaven Beaven. He nevertheless shone throughout School and was a very skilled member of the football team. In 1903 with the School picking up under Brooks not only did the number of pupils significantly increase but the Oxford University Delegacy gave a glowing report on the examinations, singling out Corless for praise. In the event he received a Senior Open Mathematical Scholarship for Sidney Sussex College, Cambridge, a Miller Exhibition, a Goodair Exhibition and another Grammar School Scholarship. As Head Boy in 1902 he also delivered the Guild Oration in Latin. In his early School career he had survived Beaven Beaven and was a good example of what could be achieved by the few who adhered to the regime.

Richard also shone at University and in 1907 he joined the Meteorological Office as Special Assistant to the Director, Sir Napier Shaw. By 1916 he had become Superintendent of Instruments and was awarded the OBE in 1918 for his vital work during the Great War. He continued to progress through the ranks, being a luminary in the Royal Meteorological Society in the 1920s and becoming Assistant Director of the Meteorological Office in 1939. Retiring in 1947 he joined the Royal Choral Society, he played the piano and pipe organ and was the Churchwarden of St Stephen's Church in Ealing for many years. He was awarded a CBE in 1953, but never forgot his roots, being an active member of the Grammar School Association from 1910 and President of the London Section from 1948. To his family whom he visited in Grimsargh until his death in 1967 he remained 'Good old Uncle Dick'.

Keith Haydon Moore

Having recently acknowledged the Centenary of the First World War it is important to recognise the contribution and sacrifice of some of the Old Boys of Cross Street who participated. One such was Keith Haydon Moore, who lived close to Winckley Square in Ribblesdale Place. Born in 1890 he attended Preston Grammar School from 1898, where he excelled as a scholar, winning several prizes in subjects as diverse as English Composition and Chemistry as well as scholarships that brought him financial assistance for his education. In 1904 he finished seventh in order of merit in the Chartered Accountants Institute examinations and went on to become a junior partner in the family firm of W. L. Moore and Son, of Winckley Square. Immediately prior to the War he was in charge of the Southport office.

He was a prime mover in re-establishing the Old Boys' Association in 1908, being appointed Treasurer two years later and becoming editor of the magazine. He was also a keen sportsman and was well-known in rugby circles, representing Preston Grasshoppers at half-back. At the outbreak of the War he was a Second Lieutenant in the Territorials and had acted as Company Adjutant. In May 1915 he set out for France as a Lieutenant with the 4th Battalion Loyal North Lancashires and was soon wounded in the wrist by a bullet during the 'great bayonet charge' by his Regiment at Festubert on 15th June 1915, unsuccessful in that the gains could not be consolidated. Having recovered at Weeton Barracks he returned to France in September and was killed on 26th November 1915 near Albert, on the Somme. He is buried in Authuile Military Cemetery and his headstone bears the inscription 'One who never turned his back, but marched breast forward'. It is difficult to find a more fitting epitaph for the sacrifice of an Old Boy from the Cross Street School.

Benjamin Harold Rayner

Benjamin Harold Rayner was born in Preston in 1886 and attended the Moor Park School from 1892 to 1899 before entering the Grammar School. He stayed only for two years before moving on to the Harris Institute, presumably for the Science

Benjamin Harold Rayner
Source not identified (*David Barrett*)

subjects, whilst simultaneously teaching at his old Moor Park School. He later gained BSc degrees from both Aberystwyth and University College, London.

From 1910 and during 1914 he was teaching Science and Maths at Dartford Grammar School when war broke out, although he did return to Preston in 1915 to marry Elizabeth Houlding. The Spring 1916 edition of the *Dartfordian* reported that 'he had the reputation of doing very thoroughly whatever he undertook', and added that 'although before the War he was not concerned with military matters, he put aside his predilections for the student life and took a commission'. In fact Rayner was one of the first amongst the School staff to sign up for military service in 1914, and he was gazetted 2nd Lieutenant in the Prince of Wales' Own North Staffordshire Regiment, serving with the 1/5th Battalion.

He was promoted to Captain but to his frustration served the first part of the War as a signalling instructor at Rugeley in Staffordshire, being responsible for the training of between four and five hundred men in each signalling course. In 1917 he was finally able to write to his Headmaster and tell him that he was excited to be going to see action at last and that it was up to him 'to make good'. He arrived in France in May and joined up with his Regiment on 8th June. Unfortunately his eagerness led to his death less than a week later, on 14th June, when during a fruitless raid at Lievin, just outside of Lens, he was blown up by a trench mortar. He was reported as 'missing, believed killed', his body was never identified or recovered and he is remembered on Panel 7 of the Memorial at Arras. It serves to remind us of the waste of life amongst the well-intentioned boys of Cross Street.

Capt Cedric Naylor relaxing on the deck of HMS *Penshurst*
The Naylor family (PGSA)

Cedric Naylor

A number of Cross Street boys joined the Royal Flying Corps, most still being cadets when the War ended, although 2nd Lieutenant Alexander Drysdale crashed his plane and was killed at Grantham in March 1918. But of the sailors John Linton Myers was not the only one to make his mark.

Possibly the most-decorated Old Boy was Captain Cedric Naylor, RN, CVO, DSO and two Bars, DSC and Bar, Mentioned in Despatches. He was born in 1891 and attended the Grammar School from 1900. Sometime later he joined the Merchant Navy, and also the Royal Naval Reserve following the outbreak of the Great War. He served on HMS *Conqueror*, a Dreadnought-type battleship which was at Jutland, and HMS *Cyclops*, originally a Merchantman but refitted for use as a Fleet Maintenance Ship and refitted again as a Depot Ship for Auxiliary Patrols based at Scapa Flow, which basically meant anything. Promoted to Lieutenant, which effectively meant Commander, he joined the Royal Naval Special Service, and was assigned duty on HMS *Penshurst*, which was a Q-Ship (Q7). These were essentially merchant vessels in this case a collier, with disguised armoury and intentions, and they were employed amongst other things to operate against enemy merchant ships and to lull submarines into a false sense of security,

Beware HMS *Penshurst*!

The white windscreen on the lower bridge concealed a 6-pounder gun at either side, a dummy boat just forward of the funnel hid a 12-pounder and the aft deck house could reveal two 3-pounders. Depth charges were released through ports in the stern.

The Naylor family (PGSA)

On board HMS *Penshurst* in a heavy sea

The Naylor family (PGSA)

enticing them to surface rather than waste a torpedo, so they could be shot at and hopefully outgunned. Naylor as Commanding Officer held the record number of successful Q-Ship actions against enemy submarines and HMS *Penshurst* was more heavily involved than any other Q-Ship. She sank two of the 11 U-Boats identified by German Naval Intelligence as having been destroyed by Q-Ships but was eventually sunk herself by U-110 although all hands were saved. Naylor must have become accustomed to having medals pinned to his chest and apart from not being awarded the VC he must have been one of the most highly-decorated Junior Officers ever to have served in the Royal Navy.

He remained in Service until 1935, and then returned for the Second World War, becoming the Commanding Officer of the Royal Navy Base Bombay, before reverting to Retired in 1945/46 and passing away in 1949. Whilst he was not well-known because of the nature of his service, he was an absolute beacon amongst the notable luminaries of the Cross Street Grammar School.

Preston Grammar School War Memorial 1914–1918
Mounted on the interior south wall of St John's Minster, Preston.
Photograph by Robin Utracik

The Preston Pals

The 'Pals' Battalions were formed shortly after the outbreak of the First World War. Being comprised entirely of volunteers they were an expedient solution to the political problem of raising an army by conscription, the regular army of 1914 being far too small to undertake a major overseas expedition. In theory the Pals would embody the spirit of their local communities and organisations, and would add the qualities of cohesion, loyalty and brotherhood to their cause. In the end, conscription became inevitable, but not before many of these Pals Regiments had been decimated, with grim consequences for their communities. Little was known about the Preston Pals until a letter appeared in the *Lancashire Evening Post* a few years ago and Andrew Mather, a retired printer, set about establishing The Preston Pals War Memorial Trust.

On 31st August 1914, Cyril Cartmell, son of the Mayor of Preston, Councillor (later Sir) Harry Cartmell, and an Old Boy of Cross Street, placed an advert in the *Daily Post*, asking for volunteers. Within 48 hours the list was oversubscribed, and 250 men then formed the 'D' Company, the 7th Battalion, the Loyal North

Lancashire Regiment. Cartmell himself served as a Captain in 'Cartmell's Company'. On the first day of The Somme, the Battalion's battle order was cancelled following the morning's catastrophes, but many were killed or wounded near Bazentin-le-Petit on 23rd July 1916. Other casualties occurred on the Somme, but on that single day the 7th Battalion as a whole lost 223 men, a lot of whom were Pals.

Amongst the Pals who embarked for France were at least 13 Old Boys: A. J. Ainsworth, Cyril Cartmell, Norman Russell Farnworth, Harold Fazackerley, Charles William Kay, Walter McIlwaine, Vincent Park, Charles Edward Parkinson, Archibald Patterson (missing from the *Preston Herald Roll of Honour*), Hugh Carnegie Rain, William Whistlecra(o)ft, John Hamilton Whitehead and Clive Whittle. Of the ones who did not return, Whittle was probably the only (Pals) Old Boy to die at Bazentin-le-Petit, whilst Parkinson was killed at Ypres a year later. Fazackerley was awarded The Military Cross and Bar but lost his life in August 1918, and the last-known to be killed in action was Kay, known as 'Penelope' and later 'Charlie' at School, on 3rd November 1918. The first and the best-known would undoubtedly have been Rain, whose father was none other than Hugh Rain, better known as Will Onda. Will, who had started out as an acrobat, became a 'musical entertainer', but more importantly a pioneer of cinema, both as a film-maker and distributor. He owned several cinemas and theatres, including the Princes, the Regent Ballroom and the Picturedrome in Brackenbury Place. Elected to the Council in 1920, he became an Alderman in 1935. Hugh Jnr died of his wounds on 27th September 1915 (the Pals' first action at Loos) before his father could arrive from the UK. He had been a Drummer in the Pals, and a clerk in civilian life, but was retrospectively described as the 'Manager for Will Onda's Animated Pictures'. The Rains and their theatres are still fondly remembered by Prestonians with links to the past.

There was no 'Pals Unit' homecoming recognition at the end of the War. They simply vanished from history until the Preston Pals War Memorial Trust began its work. In 2012 a memorial plaque was unveiled on Preston Railway Station by the Lord Shuttleworth KG, KCVO, and in 2016, exactly one hundred years after the Battle of the Somme, the Grammar School Association installed a plaque on Lochnagar Crater near La Boisselle, in memory of all the 59 Old Boys who died in the First World War, but more specifically to the memory of Clive Whittle who died on the Somme.

Clive Whittle

Clive William Cranshaw Whittle, one of three children including twin sisters, was born in 1893, and brought up in Ashton-on-Ribble, attending St Andrew's School and in 1906, Preston Grammar School in Cross Street. He left there in December 1910 and commenced as a clerk in his father's auctioneer's business. He also had an interest in the theatre and set out as a performer, appearing at the Theatre Royal as a duettist and humourist alongside his friend Harold Fazackerley. This was right at the outbreak of war, and the pals, now signed up as 'Pals', featured in the *Preston Guardian* of 26th September 1914. Their act had been greeted as 'sensational' and it was hoped that they would soon be returning home to perform again in Preston. Of course it was then believed that the War would be over by Christmas.

Clive, still a clerk when he signed up, obviously had to put his theatrical career on hold. During training at Tidworth he was confined to Barracks on a couple of occasions for relatively minor indiscretions, but on 17th July 1915 he embarked with the 7th Battalion at Folkestone for Boulogne, spending more than a year in France before having the opportunity to encounter any real action.

On 20th July 1916 he found himself at Bazentin-le-Petit, his Battalion having just marched from Henencourt Wood after a period of 'rest' at Albert. Here they held an extended line of over 1000 yards, and on that first night actually managed to shoot down a German plane with a Lewis Gun!

After three very uncomfortable days in the trench, in the early hours of the morning of 23rd July they were ordered to attack and take High Wood. There had been previous attempts by other Divisions, and now it was the turn of the 19th (including the 7th Loyals) and the 1st, the irony being that High Wood had already been taken and lost just days before.

The PGSA plaque at Lochnagar Crater
Roger Smithson (PGSA)

Word got back to Clive's family that he had been killed in the action and an article appeared in the local paper. However, at this stage there were precious few details and another month was to pass before one of Clive's surviving 'Pals' pals wrote a letter to his father John, who in turn published it in the *Preston Herald* on 26th August. The events of the attack were described in detail and obviously a wholesale slaughter had taken place. There was no sign of Whittle as dawn broke but some time later two sergeants independently confirmed that he had been shot and killed. He was awarded the 1915 Star and the British War and Victory Medals, and his name appears on a Special Memorial (no 13) in Caterpillar Valley Cemetery, Longueval, amongst 32 who are known to have been buried there.

Harold Fazackerley, the other half of the double act was likewise to perish two years later, thus bringing an end to the hopes of the *Preston Guardian* and adding another dimension to the definition of futility. There had been a price to pay for Preston Grammar School and Winckley Square.

POSTSCRIPT

The Grammar School in Cross Street certainly had more than its fair share of notable luminaries, all of whom contributed to the rich history of Winckley Square. In the same vein Winckley Square contributed much to the rich lives of these luminaries. During my time as Secretary of the Preston Grammar School Association I have had the privilege of meeting or at least communicating with the families of several of the Old Boys mentioned above, and I am in contact with some of the 'boys' who have direct links with Cross Street.

Whilst still a toddler my grandmother would take me into the then town centre every Saturday morning, ostensibly to shop but more often than not to have a look around. I would have preferred to have visited the toy shops owned by the Mears (both Old Boys of the School), but we often went to the Harris Museum, Library and Art Gallery and then to the 'cluster of buildings' on the corner of Cross Street and Winckley Square just to stand and admire them. Here she would adopt a hushed, reverent tone and I would experience a brief session of what I would now

The 'cluster', *c.*1900
Viewed from the corner of Winckley Square and Cross Street.
Sepia postcard, PDA

identify as motivational psychology. I think it was always assumed that I would go to the Grammar School, and as a result so did I, never once failing to be inspired even by an empty building! It was not difficult to imagine the boys sticking their chests out and proudly singing 'Now Thank We All Our God' in the old School Hall in April 1913 before marching in orderly fashion to the new premises on Moor Park Avenue, to await the arrival of Lord Derby and the Mayor for the opening ceremony.

The 'cluster' in the 1950s, with demolition not far away
Lancashire County Library and Information Service (PDA)

Despite young eyes it was plain to see that Winckley Square and the Cross Street Grammar School were part and parcel of the same package. They belonged together, they were mutually beneficial, and a study of their shared history ultimately confirms this. To portray it has been the intention of this monograph. What was less obvious, and flying in the face of all the prima facie 'evidence', was the invented history of the School. The true history (if known) might have been worthier and more fascinating, but it might not have attracted the same attention and there would certainly have been a need to erase the memory of the later years in Stoneygate. Perhaps the historians of the time really did believe their own tenet that Grammar Schools did not exist before Tudor times. At any rate, in terms of credibility and in raising the bar, the Tudors certainly came in useful. My delay in recounting this aspect of the story was purely down to my wish not to spoil the surprise!

Returning to the facts it is true that the Cross Street buildings might have outlived their usefulness, but what happened next beggars belief. At first the Council spent money on the Grammar School in order to let it out to the Post Office Engineering Department. After the Second World War there was a rather optimistic suggestion that it could be used as a community centre war memorial, but the lease with the Post Office ran until 1953. Prior to this in 1951 the Council then decided that it should be used for further education but in 1955, in another complete volte-face it was listed for demolition, the type of act for which the Council has always shown great aptitude. The usual excuse was made – 'historical interest but

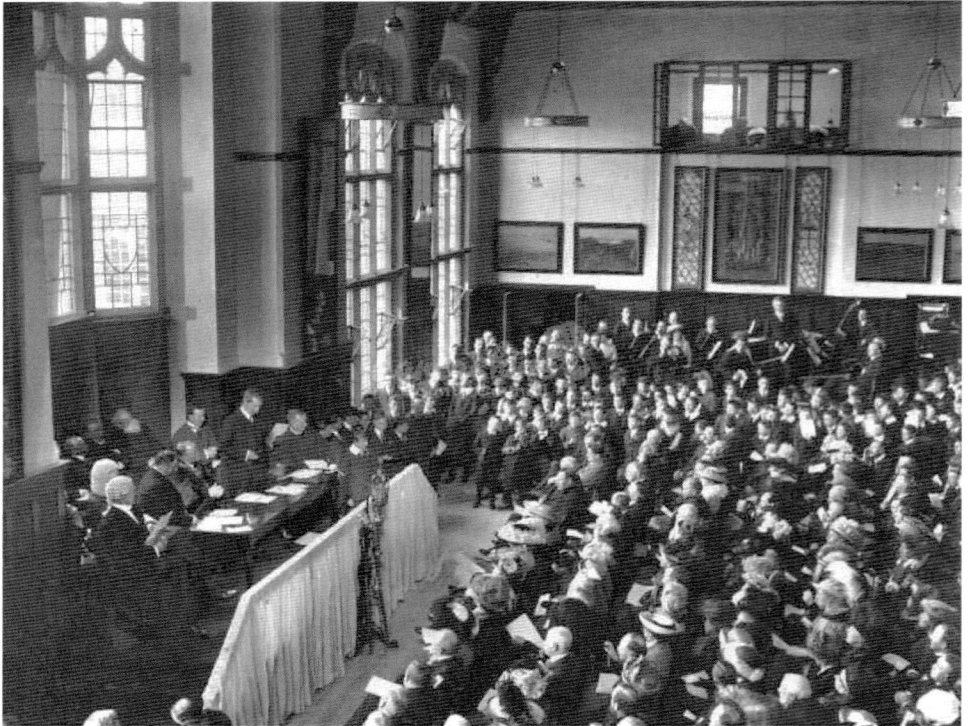

The dawn of a new era in Moor Park
The opening ceremony of the new building, on 19th April 1913. R. C. Brown's organ had not yet been installed. The School Orchestra was conducted by P. G. Coles.

MPHSSF

too far gone inside and potentially dangerous', and so it was that the cluster of beautiful buildings, the acknowledged jewel in the crown, along with William Ainsworth's Italianate Villa were simply swept away in 1957 in an act of municipal and architectural vandalism. For years the School had co-existed happily with Winckley Square and the mutual benefits had been enthusiastically embraced by both. It could be strongly argued that the success of the School had attracted the

A stark reminder of 'progress'
PDA

presence of the Catholic College. So what did the destruction of the much-admired buildings in the 'cluster' in order to make way for a modern office block, add to the prestige, the beauty and the health and wellbeing of the Square? These days they would have all been listed. It is hard not to believe that the Council simply didn't care about the Grammar School, especially when seen in the light of the political vandalism that sparked its abolition ten years later.

The relationship had been special. The divorce would be absolute.

Of course it wouldn't happen now . . .

PRESIDENTS OF THE PGS ASSOCIATION

From reforming in 1908

1908	Sir William Ascroft	1979	R. E. (Ron) Severs
1910	Sir George Toulmin	1980	W. E. Mason
1912–1925	Sir Robert Charles Brown	1981	C. Kay MBE
1925	J. M. Worthington	1982	F. W. Woodruff MBE
1927	H. P. Bee	1983	Colin Williams
1929	T. H. C. Derham	1984	Richard Sunderland
1931	W. H. Pimblett	1985	J. R. Greenhalgh
1933	F. Friedenthal	1986	J. H. Taylor
1935	W. Rigby	1987	S. Rawlinson
1937	W. Smirk	1988	Philip Ainscough
1939	J. W. Taylor	1989	Canon Jim Hamilton
1941	E. W. Wells	1990	H. Barnett
1943	Ernest Walters	1991	J. S. (James) Treasure OBE
1945	W. C. Attwater	1992	H. H. (Bert) Andrew QC
1947	Arthur Winter	1993	D. C. (David) Bunting
1949	J. Page	1994	K. W. (Keith) Nightingale
1951	F. K. Dobson	1995	L. A. (Tony) Pickston
1953	W. G. Hunniball	1996	J. A. M. (James) Bell
1955	W. T. Broadbent	1997	J. R. M. (Jim) Heppell
1957	M. Bagot	1998	C. W. (Charles) Bennett
1958	J. M. Briggs	1999	Syd Gillibrand CBE
1959	F. Hind	2000	J. K. (Keith) Hunt
1961	A. E. Willmoth	2001	G. T. (Geoff) Swarbrick
1963	A. W. Dawson	2002	Gordon Payne
1965	G. Smithies	2003	E. J. (Eric) Mills
1967	F. Whittall	2004	J. C. (John) Foster
1969	A. R. W. (Alan) Jones	2005	Stephen Sartin
1971	T. Heaps	2006	A. S. B. (Tony) Olivine
1972	John Brandwood	2007	M. F. (Mike) Tyrer
1973	C. E. Rigby MBE	2008	John Brandwood
1974	H. W. L. (Wynn) Cumming	2009–2014	John Mayson Whalley
1975	R. B. (Bob) Wade	2014–2015	Colin Monks
1976	J. Turner	2015–2017	Jim Goring (Acting)
1977	W. Whalley	2017–2019	Jim Goring
1978	Michael Johnson	31 12 1919	Date of PGSA closure

BIBLIOGRAPHY

Barrett, David. Unpublished research on Benjamin Harold Rayner (PGSA).

Berry, A. J. *The Story of Preston.* Isaac Pitman & Sons, London, 1912.

——. *Proud Preston's Story.* Toulmin & Sons, Preston, 1928.

Billington, David. *Richard Corless.* PGSA Newsletter 2010.

——. *The Myres Connection; Extract from the (unpublished) Memoirs of Professor Sir John Linton Myres (1869–1954).* PGSA Newsletter 2010.

——. *PGS and the Preston Guild Merchant.* PGSA Newsletter 2012, Guild Edition.

——. *The School Organ and the Titular Organist.* PGSA Newsletter 2012, Guild Edition.

——. *The Headmaster's Chair.* PGSA Newsletter 2012, Guild Edition.

——. *The Cross Street Mural(s).* PGSA Newsletter 2012, Guild Edition.

——. *The Preston Pals.* PGSA Newsletter 2012, Guild Edition.

——. *The Preston Pals: The Commemorative Centenary Service. The New Hoghtonian.* Issue 6, September 2016.

——. *Herbert George Ponting (1870–1935).* PGSA Newsletter 2012, Guild Edition.

——. *So Who Was Clive Whittle? The New Hoghtonian.* Issue 8, April 2017.

Brooks, Revd H. C. *Preston School Register (PGS) (Sep 1898–Dec 1899).*

Brown, Sir R. C. *Sixty-Four Years A Doctor.* George Toulmin & Sons, Preston, 1922.

Crighton, Edmund J. *Types and Shadows, A History of Preston City Parish*, Preston CP, 2015.

Douglass, Susan. *Louisa Frances Walsh. The Winckley Square Times.* Issue 7, August/September 2018.

Farrer, William (ed). *The Chartulary of Cockersand Abbey of the Premonatratensian Order.* Vol. 1 Part 2, Chetham Society New series 39. (1898).

Hadwen, Alick. Unpublished Preston Grammar School Lists/Documents.

Hardwick, Charles. *History of the Borough of Preston.* Worthington, Preston, 1857

Hebgin-Barnes, P. *Discovering the unknown: the Medieval Stained Glass of Lancashire. Vidimus.* Issue 29, May 2009.

Heppell, James R. M. *A History of Preston Grammar School.* Carnegie Publishing, Preston, 1996.

Hewitson, Anthony. *History of Preston.* Republished by S. R. Publishers Ltd. Wakefield, 1969.

Holmes, C. J. *Self and Partners (Mostly Self). Being the Reminiscences of Sir Charles Holmes.* Constable & Co, London, 1936.

Howard, Frank Esq. *A descriptive account of the historical decorations now putting up in the Grammar School, Preston.* (*The Illustrated Historic Times*, A Church of England Family Journal of Education, Literature, Science and General Intelligence. Vol. 1 No.15, Richard Birtles, London, Friday April 27th 1849).

——. *A descriptive account of the historical decorations now putting up in the Grammar School, Preston.* (*The Historic Society of Lancashire and Cheshire*, Vol. 1 (1848–1849).

Hunt, David. *The Wharncliffe Companion to Preston.* Wharncliffe Books, Barnsley 2005.

——. *A History of Preston.* Second Edition, Carnegie Publishing, Lancaster 2009.

Leach, Arthur F. *English Schools at the Reformation 1546–48.* Westminster, Constable 1896.

——. *The Schools of Medieval England.* London, Methuen & Co Ltd, 1915.

Leach, Samuel, *Old Age Reminiscences.* 1916, privately published 1923. Lancashire Archives.

Mannex, P. & Co. *The History, Topography, & Directory of the Borough of Preston.* Preston 1851.

Miller, George C. *Bygone Preston,* Provincial Newspapers Ltd, Preston, 1956.

——. *Peeps at Old Preston.* Provincial Newspapers Ltd, Preston, 1957.

Morgan, Nigel. *Vanished Dwellings.* Mullion Books, Preston 1990.

Pollard, W. *A Handbook and Guide to Preston.* (1882).

Potter, Terry. *Reflections on Preston,* Sigma Leisure, Wilmslow, 1993.

Roberts, Marian. *The Story of Winckley Square Preston.* D. J. Printing, Preston, 1988.

Sartin, Stephen, (*The People and Places of*) *Historic Preston.* Carnegie Press, Preston, 1988.

Sather, K. & L. Assoc. *Winckley Square Preston: Conservation Area Appraisal.* Altrincham, 2009.

Snape, Robert. *Objects of Utility: cultural responses to industrial collections in municipal museums, 1845–1914.* Paper, University of Bolton, 2010.

Stephen, Leslie (ed). *Dictionary of National Biography, Howard, Frank.* ed. Sidney Lee, Vol. 28, 1885–1900, London, Smith, Elder & Co, 1891.

Timmins, Geoffrey. *Preston: A Pictorial History.* Phillimore, Chichester, 1992.

Various, *The Hoghtonian.* The PGS and Association Magazine, many issues.

Whittle, P. & H. *The Commercial Directory of Preston and its Environs.* Preston, 1841.

ACKNOWLEDGEMENTS

Andrew Mather, retired printer, book designer and publisher.

Robin Utracik, Northern Studios Preston.

Aidan Turner-Bishop for initial words of encouragement.

Steve Harrison, the Friends of Winckley Square, a friend and former School, football and University colleague, who kindly wrote the Foreword at very short notice.

Professor John Insley, my oldest friend and colleague from Preston Grammar School, who provided the Introduction to the text.

Stephen Sartin, another Old Boy of PGS, for his friendship, knowledge, support and advice.

Jim Goring, President of Preston Grammar School Association, and the other members of the PGSA Executive Council, Brian Hall, Brian Rigby and Trevor Sergeant.

Jim McDowall, website originator, for helping preserve the memory of PGS.

All former Presidents and members of the PGSA, for their many years of encouragement and support.

Current and former Headmasters, Ben Corbett and Peter Cunningham, and members of staff at the Moor Park High School and Sixth Form, Preston.

Sara Park, Office Manager MPHSSF, who provided several images.

Richard Ainscough, author of *The Winckley Club*, for sound advice.

Maurice Barker, Old Boy and former PGS Master, for his report on the Head-master's Chair.

John Brome, who alerted me to the illustration of the lithograph of the gable wall in Cross Street.

Debra Kay, for her part in helping me to retrieve the Headmaster's Chair and the School Lectern, now re-presented by the PGSA to, and holding pride of place in, Moor Park High School and Sixth Form.

The staff of St Catherine's Hospice for their ongoing support of this project.

The authors of the illustrations,* who have been acknowledged individually.

* Some of the illustrations are not of the best quality but have been included on account of their historical interest and rarity.

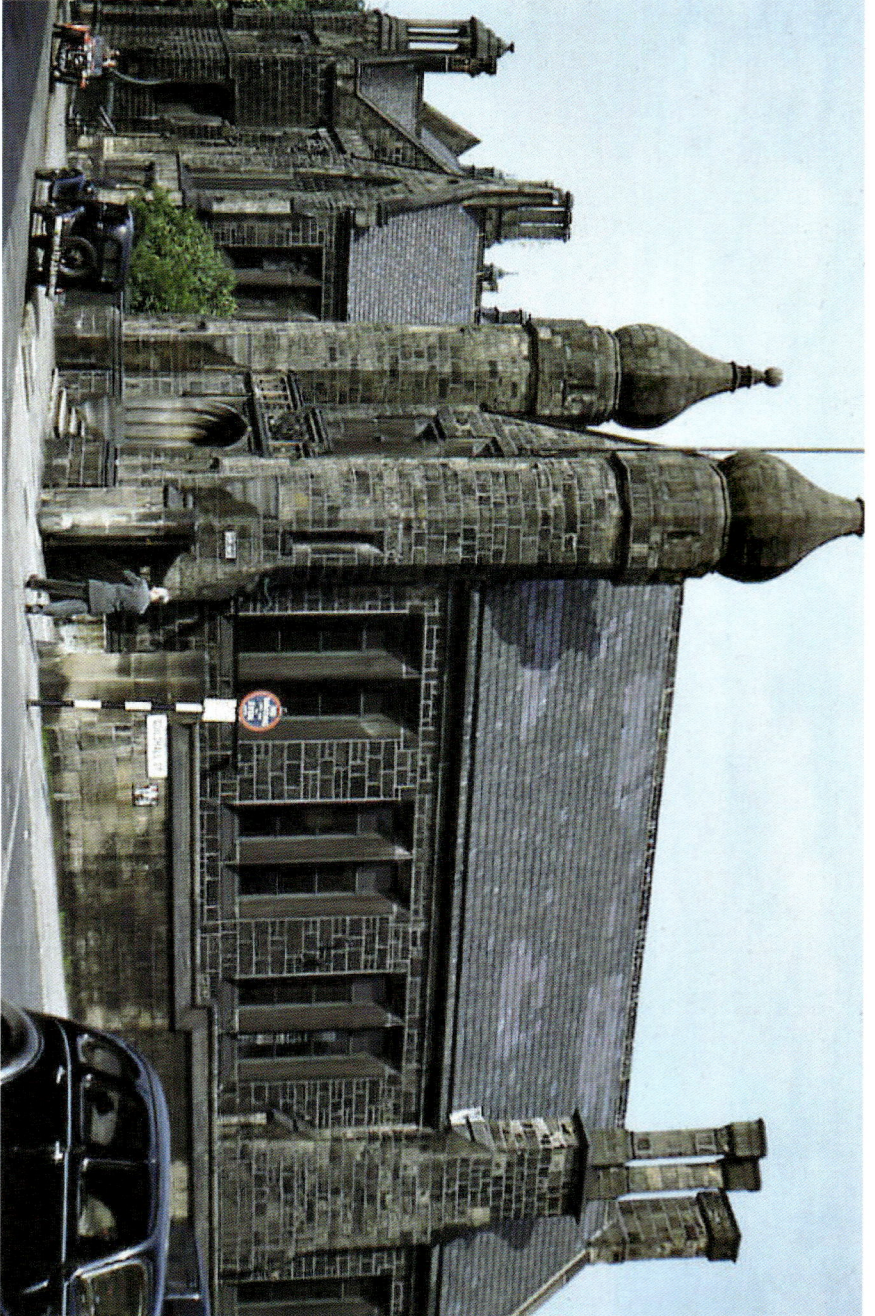

The Cross Street building in the 1950s

PGSA

Demolition of the School in 1957

In this and the previous image the pre-1950s vehicles are testament to the austerity of the post-war period.

With a touch of irony, the two Morris 8 Post Office telephone vans perfectly illustrate the adage that 'old habits die hard', the engineering department having already disappeared in a cloud of dust!

Lancashire Evening Post (PDA)

St Catherine's
hospice care

This booklet has been financed by the Preston Grammar School Association, supported by a legacy from the late Alick Hadwen.

In a day and age when most of us have been touched by cancer, all proceeds will go directly to St Catherine's Hospice to formally recognise the wonderful work being carried out there, almost unnoticed, on a daily basis.

We are all deeply grateful